My Wife Doesn't Love Me Anymore

The Love Coach Guide to Winning Her Back

Andrew G. Marshall

MARSHALL METHOD
PUBLISHING

The case histories in this book are based on couples with whom I have worked in my marital therapy practice (their identities have been changed to protect confidentiality, and sometimes two or three cases have been merged together) and individuals who have written to me via my website.

Marshall Method Publishing
London • Florida
www.marshallmethodpublishing.com

Library of Congress Cataloging-in-Publication Data is available through the Library of Congress.

ISBN: 978-0-9574297-7-2

Cover design: Gary A. Rosenberg • www.thebookcouple.com
Typeset by Troubador Publishing Ltd, Leics, UK.

Printed in the United States of America

10   9   8   7   6   5   4   3   2   1

Contents

Introduction

It is almost 10 years since the first person arrived in my marital therapy room having told their partner: "I love you but I'm not *in* love with you." As a result I wrote an article for the *Observer* newspaper in the UK about couples splitting up not because they hated each other but because one partner had fallen out of love.

The response was overwhelming and I was asked to write the book, *I Love You But I'm Not In Love With You: Seven Steps To Saving Your Relationship* (Bloomsbury). It turned out to be not just a UK phenomena: the book has been translated into German, French, Italian, Chinese, Japanese, Swedish, Greek, Turkish—in fact, 15 languages and counting. I also became the first UK-based self-help writer to be published by HCI (the US publishing giant behind the best-selling *Chicken Soup for the Soul* series).

Back in 2006, when the book was published, I thought I'd written everything that needed to be said on *I Love You But* . . . However, it was aimed at both the person who had fallen out of love *and* their partner. I didn't cover the differences between when a man falls out of love and when a woman falls out of love, because I didn't want to make generalizations about *all* women this or *all* men that. My sample of cases were all couples who were committed enough to saving their relationship to phone Relate (the UK's leading couple counseling charity), book an appointment for an initial assessment and wait the weeks and sometimes months to start ongoing counseling. However, desperate letters to my website (www.andrewgmarshall.com) told a different story—one where women and men told their partners they'd fallen out of love and either immediately or a few days later declared that the relationship was over. They couldn't 'change' their feelings, they needed 'space' and the children should 'be told.' There was 'no point' going into counselling and if the person who had fallen out of love did reluctantly agree, it was just to check the box that said 'we tried everything.' These correspondents had found my book incredibly helpful and had drawn hope from my message that you can fall back in love again, but wanted to know how to communicate this to their partner.

The more letters I received and the more stories I heard, the more I began to realize it was a completely different experience being a man told *I love you but* . . . rather than a woman. Time and again, these men were isolated and didn't know where to turn for support. They had always taken their emotional problems to their wives. Their friends might have offered a beer and the chance to take their mind off their problems but not much else. They were on their own. Worse still, these men were making simple mistakes that not only deepened their depression and anxiety but actually pushed their wives further away.

By 2010, I had set up in private practice and the majority of my clients were couples where one partner had fallen out of love. I knew I had to write a book targeted specifically at men when a male client had been so overwhelmed by panic that he'd undone all the good work of the previous session over the subsequent week. Desperate for reassurance from his wife that there was still hope, he had been using her guilt about hurting their children to try and force her to stay, I told him that short of phoning his wife a taxi, he'd done everything possible to push her out of the door. Both the husband and the wife laughed because it was horribly accurate. Sadly, I couldn't save their marriage—partly because they arrived too late, but mainly because the husband didn't need just weekly therapy but regular coaching too.

So what's the difference? Counseling, or therapy, is about helping someone open up, explore their feelings and ultimately find their own solutions. It works best when the peak of a crisis is over and the dust has settled a bit. However, my male client did not need to get in touch with his anxiety but to manage it better. And that's where coaching comes in. Coaching is about sharing knowledge (gained from previous experience in the trenches of a problem). It offers practical suggestions and helps you rehearse your messages to your partner. Ultimately, coaching is about keeping you focused and stopping you from turning a crisis into a disaster.

How to use this book

In an ideal world, if your partner has fallen out of love, you should be in couple counseling, working through the issues together as well as getting personal emotional support. In this book, I will help you decide who would be best to turn to and who you should definitely avoid. Unfortunately, we don't live in an ideal world so *I Love You But I'm Not In Love With You* can be your couple's counseling and *My Wife Doesn't Love Me Anymore* can be your personal love coach. When I counsel men face-to-face, I write down the main lessons from each session for them to take away. I've done something similar for you with the "Love Coach's Three Key Things to Remember" at the end of each chapter. Ultimately it doesn't matter which order you read the books but please don't skip *I Love You But I'm Not In Love With You* as it covers some of the techniques and ideas for saving your marriage in more depth. If you're currently holding both books in your hand (or have both e-books), I would start with *I Love You But I'm Not In Love With You*.

An Apology

I have used the word "wife" rather than "partner" in the title because I wanted to immediately indicate this book is targeted at men. However, let me be clear: this is a book for *all* men in committed relationships, whether married, living together or separated.

I'm also going to have to make blanket statements about being a man, even though I know there are countless exceptions. Having said that, there is also truth in many generalizations. So even if something strikes you as "yes but . . ." please stay with me because although you might not personally fall completely into any stereotype, it will illuminate how you might be coming across to your wife and an extreme example will often demonstrate more clearly what you might need to change.

Andrew G. Marshall
www.andrewgmarshall.com

Chapter One

Help! My wife has fallen out of love

"Fifteen days ago, my wife told me she doesn't love me anymore, that I'm her best friend but that as things are I shouldn't have any hope. I was shocked —I couldn't believe what I was hearing—and I felt like all my life was being taken from inside of me. All my dreams, hopes and future. During the last two weeks, I have hardly slept, can't eat and I'm afraid to know how much weight I've lost."

Your wife has said, "I don't love you anymore," and you're in shock. "How could this be? What does she mean? But we were supposed to be together forever? She doesn't love me?" Even if you were aware that the two of you had problems or that your marriage has been under pressure lately, you didn't think it had come to this.

And that's the problem: men don't usually keep taking the temperature of their relationship to see if it's all right. We sort of leave the love stuff to our wives. OK, we know we have to wine and dine, maybe buy her flowers on Valentine's Day and suchlike, but if we had ever thought about it, love is sort of woman's work. If there was ever a real problem, we trust that she'd tell us and we'd sort it out. Except now she's not saying "you're not doing enough around the house," or "you take me for granted," or "we never go out any more"—things that can easily be fixed. She's saying she's fallen out of love.

What's even worse than not understanding what's happened, or how to win back her love, is that you feel so completely alone. In the past, when you had an emotional problem—perhaps you'd had a quarrel with your parents or had a falling out with a work colleague—you would discuss everything with your wife and she'd either act as a go-between or help you get everything straight in your mind. Except, you can't talk to her this time. She's the problem!

If you're like most men, your friends won't be much help. They will either tease you: "Can't keep her satisfied then?" or buy you another drink. Maybe you do have a close friend who is sympathetic but he's either just as lost or he's offering well-meaning advice such as "there's plenty of other fish in the sea," that doesn't even begin to touch the edge of your despair. Meanwhile, your wife has a whole circle of friends who are there for her and who spend hours listening to the latest update about your bad behavior. Her magazines are full of advice on relationships, while yours only cover football, business and politics.

If you're lucky, your wife will be prepared to work at your marriage, sort out the problems and start again. The good news is that it is possible to fall back in love and not only repair your marriage but build a better one. If this is the case, you may like to read *I Love You But I'm Not In Love With You*. It explains how love changes over time and whether this crisis is part of moving from one phase to another or something more fundamental. It looks at the habits that we think protect love but actually undermine it and how to turn your relationship around. In addition, there are also lots of exercises that you can do together, which provide a focus for your discussions, rather than just hitting the blank wall of "I don't love you anymore."

However, there are lots of wives who say, "It's too late," or "I've been trying to sort our marriage by myself and I'm worn out." This is complete news to you. You're wondering how it's suddenly become too late and why on earth she hasn't told you sooner. Meanwhile, you're begging for another chance: "I'm sorry I didn't notice that you were so unhappy. Please, I'll change. Trust me." If you're honest you're also feeling misunderstood, resentful and taken for granted yourself: "OK so I didn't spot the problem but that's because I've been too busy busting a gut paying the bills, decorating the house and picking the kids up from after-school activities."

Alternatively, you could be kicking yourself. If you're honest you've known about the problems for a while and from time to time, you've tried a bit harder. However, somehow everything has slipped back into the old ways. If you are being truthful with yourself, maybe you did just about enough to get her off your back or maybe the relentless pressure of everyday life just took over. For whatever reason, she did not have your full attention. But now she's got it and she keeps telling you that her feelings have changed, or that she doesn't want to hurt you but it's over. Maybe you're getting the "it's best for everybody" message and the "perhaps we should separate while we're still friends" suggestion. But whatever the variations of this depressing theme, the upshot is that your wife is certain that it's over and you feel lost.

If this is your situation then this book is for you.

Is there any hope?

If I had a dollar for every time I've been asked this question I'd be a rich man. So let's start by addressing this issue head on:

> "I just want to give you an update and say thank you. I read in one of your books how I can help change my partner by changing myself. I realized my behavior had been so negative and, in turn, why would she want to be with a negative person? So I've joined a gym and work out six times a week. I socialize with everyone and I don't say no to an invite. My wife has even surprised me for New Year and Super Bowl Sunday by coming into town and spending the evening with me. Since then, she rarely goes a day without texting or calling. She's commented how calm and laid back I've become—like the person she fell

in love with. We've spent the last two weekends together and this is all by her invites or asking to come. I was shocked last weekend when we were intimate—all initiated by her. (One of her complaints, seven months ago, was that she felt like she couldn't ever be with me that way again. And when she left this weekend she said she thought she would be nervous, but it felt comfortable.) It feels as if we're headed in the right direction. Yes, we're still separated but being intimate again makes it feel like we are making strides. She's made plans to be here this coming weekend and even planned a surprise for me in a few weeks time. Anyway, I'm looking forward to whatever is next. I'm going to continue what I'm doing, but I'm not pushing anything."

So what about your relationship? Is it possible to turn it around? My answer is yes—as long as you meet at least two of the following criteria:

- *You and your wife or partner have been together for three years or more.* You need enough time to have come out of the honeymoon phase and for your relationship to have put down some solid roots. Of course, it helps to be married— because this shows a public commitment to being a couple—but some other demonstration of lasting affection, for example, buying a home together, is enough.

- *You have children together.* Nobody with children will split up lightly. However, more importantly, day-to-day discussions about your children's needs or, if you are separated, picking them up and dropping them off provides plenty of contact time and the opportunity to try out the suggestions in this book. Some people worry that they might be only staying together for the children and I have to stress that's not what I'm suggesting but learning to communicate better as parents can translate into communicating better as partners. Other people worry that they might be "using" their child or children but as most parents' relationships often reach "I love you but . . ." because of the stress of bringing up kids, it seems only fair that they provide an opportunity to save it too.

- *You truly love her and want to win her back.* If it is just your pride that has been wounded or you're worried what friends might think, you will not have either the generosity needed for my program nor the determination to keep going through the setbacks. Although your relationship can be saved, the journey ahead is not going to be easy. It involves learning a lot about yourself (some of it might be hard to accept) and making lasting changes (rather than a quick fix and hoping for the best).

- *You don't panic.* This is perhaps the toughest criterion. Of course you're going to panic. Your wife doesn't love you anymore, she's threatening to take half of everything you own and you're going to be a part-time dad! However, the more you panic, the more you will do stupid things that push her further away. I've got lots of techniques to help you be calm, rational and focused, but it will take commitment and determination from you too. In my experience, more relationships break down at this point because of the husband's panic than the wife's determination to leave. Please remember this when you're feeling low.

Six worst reactions to discovering your wife doesn't love you

Hearing your wife say that she doesn't love you is horrible. You're bound to be upset and you will have probably said and done things that you now regret. In the long run it doesn't really matter how you reacted to her initial declaration (unless we're talking violence and I doubt that). What *really* counts is how you have behaved in the subsequent discussions—during the hours, days and weeks afterward. In many cases, women change from "I love you but I'm not in love with you," into "I don't love you any more," into "it's over," because men fall into one or more of the following traps:

Dismissive

It seems so incredible that your wife doesn't love you and it is so difficult to get your head around the idea, that you've dismissed or downgraded the whole issue. Perhaps you've tried to tell your wife that it hasn't been that bad (because you don't want the tone to be completely negative) or tried to get her to remember all the good times you've had in the past (because you want her to have a balanced view of your whole relationship not just the bad times). Maybe you've just gone quiet and hoped it would get better or it was just a difficult patch. Alternatively, you might have tried to cheer her up: "It's been tough with me working away so much but it won't be for much longer," or "It's not surprising considering that your mother has been ill."

Why this is a mistake: Your wife will either feel that you've not heard her or that you've not taken her seriously. Either way, this is a disaster. She will feel hurt, taken for granted and possibly angry but, worse still, she will feel that you aren't listening to her now so what chance is there of you listening to her and changing in the future? You will have confirmed her doubts.

Yes, but . . .

You accept that mistakes have been made—and there are lots of things that you regret—but in your haste to sort things out, you've not really told her any of this. Time and again, men assume their wives know what they're thinking—after all, it's been going around and around in their heads—but the words have not formed on their lips and been spoken. If they have, they have used the "yes but..." formula. By this I mean, "*Yes* I know I should have come with you to the exam for our daughter *but* there was an emergency at work," or "*Yes* I have been spending too much time on the golf course *but* I work hard and need to unwind." This is a better strategy than the previous one—flatly dismissing her complaint—but only just!

Why this is a mistake: Of course, there are lots of valid reasons for what's been going on—and at other times it would be perfectly valid to bring them up—but at this precise point, it sounds like you're making excuses or that you're not giving enough recognition to her unhappiness.

Running yourself down

You have been taking all the blame saying, "I've been a complete and utter fool. I've taken you for granted, behaved badly and don't deserve your love." Maybe you've thrown in half a dozen complaints that she hasn't mentioned and remembered all the put-downs from school or the times that you upset your parents too. No wonder you're feeling low, depressed and anxious. However, on the plus side, you have taken her complaints seriously.

Why this is a mistake: It's not so much that you've given her extra ammunition to throw at you and half a dozen new reasons to leave but you've made her feel a bit of a bastard (how could she kick a man when he's down?) or angry (because she feels that everything has to be about you or that her words have been twisted) or simply sad (because she didn't mean to hurt you). Whatever her reaction, she's going to either be driven further away or just feel pity—and who wants that? Worse still, people who overdramatize and catastrophise become completely overwhelmed and end up doing little more than lying on the sofa with their head in their hands and wailing. In other words, you're not going to change, there's no hope and she's better off leaving.

Talking about your love for her

She might not love you, but you're still desperately in love with her. There's nothing wrong with that. In fact, it's brilliant because it will give you the drive and determination to keep going through the dark times. The problem is telling her— again, and again, and again.

Why this is a mistake: When we say "I love you," we're sort of expecting the other person to say "I love you too," or "I love you more than you do," or "I'll love you till the stars fall from the sky." She knows what you want to hear but you're just reminding her that she doesn't love you. Worse still, this strategy is making her feel depressed or a "bad" person for not returning your love. With each declaration, you're building a brick wall with your overflowing love on one side and her empty heart on the other. I know this a lot to ask but please, please, please don't mention the subject of love again until she brings it up.

Trying to talk sense into her

Splitting up is going to devastate the kids, you will have to sell the house and it will take her years, if ever, to find love again. Surely, it would be best to try and work on your relationship? There is a lot of sense in this approach—that's what makes it a much better response than the others but it can also be a particularly dangerous trap.

Why this is a mistake: There are two problems with this

strategy. Firstly, she is talking from the heart (about her emotions, feelings and heartache) and you're talking from the head (about facts, opinions and beliefs). In effect, you're speaking two different languages. So you're bound to see things differently, disagree and become angry with her. Worse still, in your rational mind, if you present the facts one more time or gather the evidence slightly differently, she will have to see sense. So you try over and over again—which brings us to the second problem with this strategy. After so many discussions that either turn nasty or go around in circles, she will begin to believe that you're not supposed to be together simply because you're such different people. In effect, not only does this strategy not work but it provides her with more ammunition for leaving you.

Going for a quick fix

Men are trained to fix problems. So if your wife tells you she's fallen out of love, you look for a remedy: flowers and chocolates or a trip to Venice or maybe some expensive jewelry. And why not? These grand gestures have worked before. The other great advantage of this strategy is that it offers the illusion of solving the problem on the spot—just get out your credit card—and when your world is torn in two, that is very tempting indeed.

Why this is a mistake: Women tend to solve problems in a different way than men. They want to unload, examine their feelings and talk over the issues. From these free-flowing discussions, a possible answer might emerge or maybe while she's talking she'll realize the problem was not such a big deal and just being heard is enough. So imagine her reaction when she's just getting going but you're not listening because you're on the computer comparing prices for a trip on the Orient Express. At best she thinks you're rude but at worst she will believe you are not taking her problems seriously or that you are trying to buy her off. Worse still, you've most probably thrown money around or made grand gestures before (like doing all the ironing for a month) and these haven't really changed anything beyond the short term. So the last thing that you need is another quick fix that will see you back here again in a few months time.

Six best reactions to discovering your wife doesn't love you

I would be very surprised if you didn't make one of the mistakes outlined above—probably more. But don't worry or get angry with yourself—that will change nothing. The important thing is to stop the unhelpful behavior and substitute it with as many of the following helpful strategies as possible:

Acknowledging

It is really simple. When your wife seems angry or sad, you don't pretend that it hasn't happened or try and cheer her up. You say: "I can see you're angry with me," or ask her, "Why are you feeling so sad?" Your fear is that by acknowledging her pain, you will encourage her to become more upset or whatever other feeling. And you're right, in the short term, you will probably get a burst of anger, tears or recriminations. Don't worry if you can't pinpoint her feelings—for example, if you say frustrated and she felt rage. She will soon correct you.

There is another type of acknowledging and it sounds so weird or just plain stupid that many men dismiss it without another thought. So what is it? You simply acknowledge what has been said (rather than identifying the feelings behind them) by repeating back her last sentence or the main points of her message. For example, "I moaned about coming home early to look after the kids."

Why this works: Whether you are acknowledging the feelings or the words, you will make your wife feel that she is heard—rather than just rattling off words into a black hole. If you can identify her feelings, she will think that you are interested in her emotions (rather than just trying to keep everything nice) and therefore interested in her. Even if you guess incorrectly what she's feeling, she will at least feel that you are interested. Maybe she will get angrier, sadder or throw a few more insults at you (because acknowledging feelings can temporarily bring them to the surface) but firstly, it burns them out and secondly, you've probably learned a bit more about how she really feels. So I can't say it often enough: acknowledge, acknowledge, acknowledge and if you are ever in doubt at what to do over the next few difficult weeks—just try to identify the feeling or repeat back the last part of her sentence.

Even better, try both. For example, "You're feeling angry because I never take the initiative to plan anything nice."

Exploring

This concept is basically acknowledging on steroids. You don't just show her that you have heard her but ask her questions, so that you truly can UNDERSTAND her. For example: "You're angry because I never took the initiative. How did that make you feel?" She might reply: "It made me feel taken for granted." Don't defend yourself or try and put the record straight, just ask another question: "Were there other times I took you for granted?" Good questions start with: Who, Why, What, When, Where and How? For example: "What would you have liked me to do?" or "When did this start?" or "Why was this so painful?" (You might, for example, learn that she felt taken for granted by her parents and that's why she felt so let down when you did the same.)

Why this works: There are two advantages to this strategy. As you will probably have guessed by now, it will make her feel heard, taken seriously and provide a glimmer of hope that things could be different. However, more importantly, you will get a better idea of what has gone wrong and see the beginnings of a way forward to save your marriage. This strategy is crucial. Basically, you can never do too much exploring.

Check it out

It is important to double-check that you have heard correctly.

This is because when she is saying something painful your mind will be racing, interpreting and trying to find solutions. Not only can this mean that you will miss some vital piece of information but you can jump to conclusions—possibly the wrong ones. For example, she might feel that you insult her in public. Before you write this off as just banter with friends where you might poke fun at her (in a nice way of course) ask her: "Can you give me any examples?" Maybe she means that you contradict her opinions when you visit your parents (because lively debate is what happens in your family) but it makes her feel unsupported.

Why this works: In many ways saving your marriage is not about trying harder (unless you have been a complete slob and done nothing around the house) but being smarter and targeting your efforts. In other words, you are putting your energy into areas that will really count, for example, around the family dinner table rather than in gatherings of friends. And that's doubly helpful because smarter is not only more effective than running around in circles exhausting yourself by changing everything, but it can be sustained over the long term. There is another advantage of checking it out: it will stop your mind spinning out of control (and panicking) because you will ask: "Did you say you have never loved me?" and she will clarify: "I have wondered if I truly loved you or whether it was an infatuation." I know they are both horrible but there is a big difference between thinking something and believing it. Fortunately, checking it out allows you to register the difference and not exaggerate and start to panic again.

Imagine every word she says is true

The previous positive strategies have been relatively straight-forward but this one is really tough. However, if you can pull it off, it is incredibly powerful. So how does it work? Forgive me if I state the obvious. We see the world through our own eyes and experience it through our own emotions. Our interpretation of an event will always be filtered through our own particular lens. However, someone else, who has an entirely different history, will have a different take. For example, what might seem like a horrible row to you might be trying to sort out a pressing problem to your wife. It is very easy to get wedded to our view of the world and to discount or downgrade everyone else's.

What's more, because we have 100 percent access to our motivations, what we do makes perfect sense to us. For example: "I don't mean to frustrate my wife by walking away during an argument, I simply want to avoid things turning really nasty—especially in front of the kids. It's not like I don't want things to be better." Through this lens, it is easy to think: "Here she goes again. Is this going to solve anything?" So you put mental brackets around her complaints—for example, she says: "You don't listen," and you mentally add, "I do until you start nagging" and because—through your eyes—you do listen, you can downgrade her complaint (because through your eyes it's not true) or dismiss it, "What do you expect if you keep nagging me?'

This positive strategy turns this everyday experience on its head. Instead of looking through your own eyes, I want you to put your interpretations to one side and remove all the justifications, explanations and brackets and imagine what your wife says is the truth, the whole truth and nothing but the truth—because through her eyes it is TRUE.

So stand in her shoes and imagine every word she says is true: What would you like to change about your behavior?

Why this works: It is like sitting right next to your wife and being 100 percent on her side. It not only gives you a fresh perspective but also some important strategies for solving this crisis. However, there is also a hidden benefit to this strategy: if you give your wife the gift of imagining every word she says is true and really understanding her, she is more likely to pay you the same compliment and return the favor. If you're finding this hard and perhaps falling into the "yes but . . ." trap then please stop for a second. If you truly love her, doesn't she deserve the respect of you imagining that, for her, what she says is true?

Processing

With these positive strategies, I have asked you to listen, acknowledge, ask questions and then ask even more questions. I have also asked you not to justify, explain, contradict or try and find solutions. I know this is tough but you are about to get your opportunity to defend yourself.

So what is processing? Well, instead of giving a knee-jerk reaction to your wife's complaints, promising to change or going for the quick-fix, I want you to sleep on what she's said or at the very least go for a walk and think it through. Afterward, tell her the main conclusions that you've drawn from your conversation together and what you plan to do to rectify the situation. When she's had the chance to correct your interpretation of her complaints and comment on your suggested remedies, you can report back your feelings, for example: "I'm really upset that you think..." or "I really love you and I want to make things better." You can then give your side of the situation, for example: "I've been working so hard because I thought it was what you wanted," or "I have been a good father because I did this.'

Why this works: Not only have you listened but you've gone away and thought about what your wife has said. This is probably the opposite of what happened in the past (or if you did listen and think about the problem, you did not share your thought process so she imagined that her words had gone in one ear and out the other). Moreover, with time and reflection, you are most likely to come up with the beginnings of a well-made plan for rescuing your relationship (more about this later in the book) rather than panicking and pushing her further away.

Getting help

Men are brought up to be self-reliant and that's great; it's one of the things that women find really admirable about us but it can also drive them mad. If your wife has a problem, she will talk it through with friends or seek expert help. So in her mind, if you've had some problems (drinking too much, erectile dysfunction, depression etc.) but have either denied them or told her that you can sort them out yourself, your self-reliance can be translated into either stupidity (and who wants a stupid husband?) or worse still that you don't love her enough to get help (so why should she love you back?).

Even if there are no background issues that have undermined her love for you, you'll need advice (for avoiding silly mistakes), a fresh perspective (to help you see things through your wife's eyes) and general support (to cheer you up when you're feeling down). So where should you get help? Speak to your doctor so he or she can help you decide if you need help for depression or anxiety. Your doctor might also be able to refer you for counseling. For a sounding board and support, I think the best person to choose would be your sister (if you have one). Even if she is not particularly close, this could be a chance to change all that. She will be able to give a female perspective. She will know your wife well and have watched the two of you interact. My second choice is your mother. However, she will most likely be 100 percent on your side, which sounds great but there is a downside. Through a mother's eyes, you are perfect just the way you are (which is why you love her but it doesn't make her the most dispassionate observer). My next choice would be a close female friend of your wife, someone who knows you both well and can help explain your wife's feelings (but hopefully minus the anger and the barbed comments). However, she will probably have divided loyalties. My final choice would be a sensible married male friend—hopefully one who has survived marital upsets but is still married. You don't need a bitter "all women are bitches" approach.

Finally, avoid any warm but unattached women. I know it is nice to have a boost to your ego from another woman, especially when you're being told that you're rubbish, but a shoulder to cry on can easily turn into a mouth to kiss, and that will definitely ruin your chances of saving your marriage.

Why this works: Getting help is solid evidence that you are taking your wife seriously and offers the opportunity of change. It will also stop you from panicking and help keep up your morale. Don't worry if you can't find someone who is truly helpful (rather than just a vaguely supportive friend who takes you out for a beer) because this book has plenty of ideas to keep you focused and moving forward.

In general, there is no downside to getting help but please process your wife's complaint first. Otherwise, you won't be able to properly explain what's been going on. There is also a risk of firing off requests in all directions rather than finding the right person and, for example, consulting three different experts at the same time (who are bound to give conflicting advice) or telling everybody you know (which your wife might consider disloyal).

Coping with your panic

It is all very well for me to stress the importance of keeping calm, listening and processing what your wife is saying but what if every word pushes you further over the edge?

"Last week, my wife repeated to our counselor that she just wants the marriage to end and the counselor has now said we need to discuss an amicable separation. What is really strange, to me at least, is that my wife says she has no idea what she wants, only that she doesn't want me. What can I do? I'm at my wit's end as I try to avoid getting upset and not telling her how much I love her (as she says this puts too much pressure on her). Other times, I just get so angry that I just seem to get into a childish rage and then afterward promise her everything will be OK. I'm becoming increasingly miserable (but wouldn't actually claim to be depressed) and full of woe to the point that I have told my wife that she'd be better off without me and I'd be better off dead.'

It is important that you begin to recognize the first signs of panic or that everything is becoming too much. It might be that your chest feels tight, a sinking feeling in the pit of your stomach, your breathing is getting faster and shallower, a splitting headache or you just feel generally stressed. When your body is telling that you can't cope, please use one of these six strategies:

Concentrate on your breathing

If you are alone put both hands flat against your diaphragm (which you will find just under your ribs). Feel your chest rising and sinking. Try and slow down your breathing and take deeper breaths. If you are not alone, and don't want to attract attention by placing your hands on your diaphragm, just focus on the air going in and out of your nostrils. Breathe deeper and slower. Keep this up for five minutes or until you feel calmer.

Burn off some excess energy

If you're like a caged tiger or simply can't think straight, get out of the house and do some exercise. My favorite is going for a run as I think fresh air and being out of your normal surroundings gives you a fresh perspective. However, you may prefer to go for a swim, use a rowing machine or do weights at the gym. Ultimately, the choice is yours but the point is to get the blood pumping and the adrenaline out of your body.

Keep a diary or start a blog

It is much better to pour all your worries and overthinking into a diary than to burden your wife with every twist and turn of your private thoughts. Instead of letting a million and one questions go around and around your head, put them down on paper or a screen. This will not only distance you a little from your panic but you may find that some answers might appear in your ramblings. It is also helpful to return to your diary and re-read it. Hopefully, you will discover that you're making progress and although today might be bleak, it's better than yesterday or two weeks before. A variation on this theme is to keep an online blog as other people's comments will make you feel less alone.

Speak to one of your supporters

You might think that if you could just speak to your wife maybe she could reassure you or give you some hope and everything will be OK, but when you're panicking the conversation is unlikely to go well. So pick up the phone or send an email to your supporter: she or he can be a dumping ground for all your fears and help you get everything back into proportion. For example, you may think you would feel better if she was "just having an affair," but you most likely wouldn't. Similarly if you are tempted to force a particular issue— because not knowing is making you crazy—your supporter will help you stop and consider if you are in danger of making matters worse.

Plan for a better future

Instead of kicking yourself for what you've done wrong in the past, focus on what you need to do to make things better. At the moment, you might not have many ideas but this book is full of them. So instead of panicking, start reading. There are simply hundreds of self-improvement or self-help titles. There is a recommended reading list at the end of this book.

Step away

If you're in the middle of a discussion or an argument with your wife and you can feel yourself beginning to get really angry (not just regular anger, but the kind of rage where you say stuff you will regret later), in danger of sobbing, begging her to stay or becoming aggressive and pushing for "answers," please step away. Tell your wife that you need a break and leave the room. Maybe you'd like to try out one of my other coping strategies and either return after 10 minutes to half an hour, or text and tell her you're OK. Maybe you'd like to continue the conversation at this point, make an appointment to talk at another time or simply ask to drop the subject. There is no right or wrong approach but please try to avoid the unhelpful behaviors that push her away.

Love Coach's Three Key Things to Remember:

- More relationships end because of a husband's panic than a wife's determination to leave.

- Listen to your wife: really listen to what she has to say.

- Think everything through before you act.

Chapter Two

Why doesn't my wife love me?

"I could tell something was wrong, so I asked my wife and she told me that she feels we've always been just best friends and also that all of her life she feels like she has been someone else (in a relationship) instead of being herself (single) and her own person. I immediately asked a million questions including 'why?' and 'how can I fix this?' I have since pulled the reins back and given her the space that she has asked for. I'm in the Navy and currently deployed overseas, so I stopped calling and writing every day as we have done for the past six months. Now, when I finally do talk to her, all I want is to ask her all of these questions again and her exact same response for everything is always 'I don't know.'"

You've begun to wrap your head around the idea that your wife doesn't love you anymore but what you can't understand is *why*? After all, it is not so long ago that she stood at the altar or in front of a justice of the peace and all your family and friends and promised to love you for better or worse, for richer or poorer, come what may. No wonder you keep asking yourself why. No wonder you get more and more frustrated when she can't give you a satisfactory answer.

It could be true that she simply doesn't know why or when she started falling out of love. It has happened so gradually, with one disappointment piled on another, that she really can't point to one single event or reason. She just knows that she's deeply unhappy and can't go on anymore.

Alternatively, she *does* know but doesn't want to hurt you even more and therefore is either hiding behind "I don't know" or sugar-coating everything to the point that her answers are meaningless.

Sometimes, she will be able to explain—like in the letter above—her problem. In this case that she can't be "her own person." Unfortunately, her answer just doesn't make any sense to you. It's not as though you're stopping her from doing anything (and maybe you have even gone out of your way to support a particular project).

Perhaps, you do understand her complaint. Perhaps it's that, "you've not done enough around the house," or "you've never taken the initiative and planned anything," but you've no idea why these reasonably straightforward problems have drained all the love out of your relationship. Worse still, it certainly doesn't explain why your wife won't give you a chance to sort these problems out.

No matter which of these scenarios your relationship falls into, you're still stuck because if you can't understand why, how can you begin to fix anything? It might seem that you're in a hole with no way to climb out but don't worry. I've seen thousands of marriages and long-term relationships, and whatever the individual circumstances, there has been one central overriding reason for a wife (or a husband) falling out of love: poor communication.

How to diagnose what's really gone wrong with your marriage

Despite the fairy tales and the myth of soul partners, it is impossible for two people to live happily ever after and in complete harmony without falling out from time to time. That's why you need to be able to sort out small complaints (so they don't fester into resentment) and to negotiate when bigger conflicts arise (so your marriage does not fall into the trap where one of you wins and the other loses). Unfortunately, we are not taught about good communication at school and if your parents swallowed confrontation, or one of them squashed down the other, or they fought like cat and dog, you won't have learned at home to resolve problems either. So what happens when two people have disagreements? There are three common but unhelpful reactions:

Being Passive

With this communication style, your opinions, needs and wants are of no importance. So you will either deny them outright: "I don't care, you choose," or you will prioritize your partner's needs over yours: "You've had a long, hard week and you need to relax on the weekend," (even though personally you're bored with staying in and watching TV every Saturday night). Relationships where one, or both, partners are suppressing their needs can be very happy—at least on the surface. There are certainly no arguments but being a people pleaser can have a terrible long-term cost. If you've always done what other people want, you can lose touch with your own needs, or feel that you're only loved if you're "nice" or "agreeable" and do what other people expect (and therefore stop being your own person).

If this is you: On the surface, going along with what your wife wants seems a great strategy. Who doesn't want to get their own way? Of course, she will love you if you'll do anything for her! Except it's only a small step from being considerate to being a doormat. No relationship where one partner is in charge and the other trots a couple of paces behind is happy in the long run. When a wife always gets her own way (and the man is passive and swallows his opinions, needs and wants) she will begin to wonder who her husband truly is and, more worryingly, she will lose respect for him. Worse still, when she loses respect, she will start behaving badly and taking him more and more for granted. Meanwhile, he finds himself "walking on eggshells" so he doesn't trigger another bout of scorn, burying his needs even deeper and making her respect him even less.

If this is your wife: It is perfectly possible for her to jog along for years in the passive role. Especially if making other people happy makes her happy. In effect, your wife has been trading any short-term benefits from getting her own way (for example, going to the theater on a Saturday night) for the middle-term benefit of a harmonious house. However, over time, there are only so many times you can swallow your own needs without feeling that you don't count and becoming disillusioned with your marriage.

Being Domineering

With this communication style, your opinions, needs and wants are of *supreme* importance and your partner's are of little or no importance (or more likely, you've never really stopped to think about them and have therefore down-graded or ignored them). Alternatively, you might have convinced yourself that your opinions are "right" and your partner is "wrong." So, of course, you *need* to buy an expensive car (after all, you have to do hundreds of miles for work and your back would act up in an inferior model) while your wife will need to wait for the kitchen to be remodeled (after all, the appliances still work and it was only done 10 years ago). Some people call this communication style aggressive because it can be achieved by shouting, getting angry or being sarcastic and putting your partner down (so they begin to believe that their opinions, needs and wants truly are of no importance). However, I meet just as many people who get their own way without being overly aggressive. They just do what they want and damn everybody else (for example, by going out and buying the car without really talking it through with their partner). They may then bribe their partner, "Let me have my own way and I'll give you sex," sweet-talk them round, "Pretty please" or make them feel guilty "You don't care about my bad back."

If this is you: If your wife has let you have your own way, no wonder you've been so happy and in love. Unfortunately, she hasn't got such a great deal herself. These kinds of marriages can work for a long time—especially if your wife has been getting some of her needs met by your children (who make her feel her opinions and feelings do count). Often there is a seemingly small event—like you buying a power tool—which will tip what she sees as your general selfishness into being unloving. This will seem baffling to you—because the power tool only cost 100 dollars! However, she has been working on the unspoken deal—which she may not even have articulated to herself previously—"If I sacrifice my needs, he will really love me and therefore give me what I need." Suddenly she has realized the math doesn't add up: "He gets all that . . . and I only get this..." I know this is tough because if someone doesn't tell you what they want, how can you second-guess? (However, little girls are taught that if they are nice, other people will be nice to them. So don't be angry with her or take it personally because this behavior goes right back to her childhood.) Unfortunately, in her mind, by buying the power tool, you've broken the unspoken deal and she will never get what she truly wants.

If this is your wife: You would have thought that getting her own way would make her happy but this is not always the case. I'm afraid I'm going to make another sweeping generalization: While little boys are taught to win (sometimes at any costs), women are taught to cooperate and be more sociable (and therefore be more aware of other people's feelings). So while a man might feel getting his own way is his due (because his mother made him feel like the king of the castle), a woman is more likely to feel ambiguous about always coming out on top. First, she will see the cost to her partner and feel guilty but second, and more importantly, she is probably feeling a "bad" person or "mean and horrible" because you "let her" trample all over you. The end result is she might get her needs met but she stops liking herself—or how she behaves in your marriage.

Swinging between being passive and domineering

This communication style comes in two forms. Firstly, you can alternate between being passive (and downplaying your opinions, needs and wants) and being domineering (and downplaying your partner's opinions, needs and wants). Often these are around specific parts of your life. For example, a woman can be domineering about a couple's social life (so that there is plenty of time to see her family but little to see yours) but passive about how money is spent in the house (so she is afraid to ask or closes her eyes to where the money comes from). Meanwhile, a man can be domineering, for example, about being allowed to flirt with other women at parties, "it's just a bit of fun" but be passive when it comes to issues about the children, "that's her domain." More frequently, someone will be passive most of the time and let their partner be in charge until something makes them snap. At that point, they become domineering and shout, browbeat or sulk until they get their own way. More often than not, their partner is so shocked that they back down right away, not because they think their partner has a good case but because they want to avoid a scene. This of course just stores up future resentment.

The second form of this communication style combines being both passive and domineering at the same time. The most common version is called passive aggressive. When someone is asked to do something, they immediately agree. So it seems, at least on the surface, that their needs, wants and opinions are of little importance. However, underneath the pleasant exterior, they are seething because they *do* think their needs, wants and opinions are important. For example, a wife will ask her husband to redecorate the spare bedroom because her mother is coming to stay. He doesn't want to spend his weekends doing DIY and doesn't want her mother to come and stay anyway, but he doesn't tell her this. Instead, he agrees to do the work to her face but then quietly sabotages it. He has to watch the Grand Prix on TV or he gets drunk on Saturday night and is too hungover to make a start on Sunday. The alternative version is domineering but in a passive way. Once again the needs of the person asking is paramount but they pretend to be passive. For example, they will play the martyr, "poor me" or make their partner feel guilty, "I do so much for you and all I ask is this one little thing." Women often bribe their husbands by "rewarding" them with sex, while men will buy their way out of trouble with presents or expensive outings.

If this is you: If you can't say no directly to your wife and use passive aggressive behavior to get your own way, this is very destructive to a marriage. Often neither of you feels powerful; she will think you are in charge (because you are always digging in your heels) and you will think she's in charge (because she sets the agenda and your only influence is negative). She will be frustrated, angry and your relationship will feel like a constant battle. If you are being domineering but in a passive way, this is equally frustrating for your wife and if you are constantly behaving like a little boy (whining, wheedling and tearful) she will lose respect. Many wives will say: "I don't need another child, I need a husband."

If you swing between being straightforwardly passive and then domineering, you risk combining the worst of both communication styles.

If this is your wife: A lot of women pride themselves on being cleverer than their husbands: "I always get my own way because I make him feel it was all his idea," or "I can twist him around my little finger." However, deep down, I don't think these women respect their husbands or, if they are being honest, really want to be so manipulative.

Lots of marriages work perfectly well where one partner is domineering in one sphere and passive in another. However when circumstances change, for example, after the birth of a child or when the children leave home or a partner has an affair, the balance of power will shift and what seemed tolerable before is no longer acceptable.

Why communication is so important

There is an alternative to being either passive, domineering or some combination of both. It is called being assertive. In this communication style *both* parties' needs, wants and beliefs are of *equal* importance. Not only does each partner ask (rather than demand or manipulate) but they listen to their partner's requests too. So how can you be assertive and still deal with disagreements or competing needs?

- Negotiate and find a middle way. For example: "Let's go to the party but leave early."

- Trade with each other. For example: "I'll go to your party if you'll look after the children so I can go out with my friends next week."

- One of you will back down (but only after feeling truly heard) because the other person's case is stronger. For example: "Even though I hate your work's outings, going to the party is really important for your promotion prospects and I want to support you."

As you can see, assertive behavior not only avoids the traps of resentment, losing sight of your own needs or lessening your respect for your partner—but the open and honest dialogue allows you to solve day-to-day problems too. More importantly, it raises the prospect of your marriage being truly different in the future. In the next chapter, where I cover how to win back your wife, I will explain more about being assertive.

Sex and falling out of love

In many ways, sex is all about communication. When initiating sex (either by asking for it directly or some signal like a hand sneaking across the bed) many couples end up with "I love you but . . ." because one partner has been too domineering and the other too passive.

> *"My wife and I had an argument in September that was in front of some friends. She later told me the devastating words: 'I love you but I'm not in love with you'. We have been married for nine years, together for 11 and we have two young kids. After our fight, we were intimate once the following week and none since. She would not even kiss me until the last two weeks and I have to instigate... and it has only happened a couple of times. I am having a terrible time with the whole mess. I don't understand how we went from being intimate*

three to four times a week for 11 years until our fight in September and now she has no interest. I am in the best shape of my life and other women have taken notice, but not my wife. I just don't know what else to do."

When you are too domineering: I'm not suggesting that you have been too forceful or aggressive in the bedroom and just took what you wanted and forgot about your wife's pleasure. Of course that wouldn't make for a happy marriage, but most men are domineering in a subtler way. What I'm talking about is focusing on your need for sex and either downgrading your wife's reluctance, "She always enjoys it once we get going," or dismissing it, "She never wants it and if I didn't push we'd never have it."

Men who are too domineering will either pester their wife until she backs down and gives in to keep the peace, sulk or create a bad mood in the house. I've also known men to threaten their wives: "There are plenty of women who would be happy to sleep with me."

Sometimes women do agree to sex (and give in to their husband's desire) rather than feel their own desire (and actively seek sex) but get turned on during foreplay. In the short term, this is fine but in the long term these women lose sight of what turns them on and slowly but surely sex becomes routine or boring. When a wife just goes along with her husband's needs (because it's Saturday night or Sunday morning) rather than feeling turned on herself, sex becomes something for him, instead of a shared pleasure.

Eventually, pestering for sex builds a wall of resentment between a couple. Meanwhile, the husband thinks the marriage is OK because they are still having sex. Unfortunately, he has been so focused on maintaining the quantity of sex, that he has been ignoring how cold his wife has become and how empty he feels after he has ejaculated.

When you are too passive: You are a kind and considerate lover but you have been so concerned with giving your wife pleasure that you have downgraded or ignored your own needs. Once again, in the short term, there is nothing wrong with this level of generosity. Unfortunately, over time, you can lose sight of your own desire or be so polite that lovemaking becomes passionless. As one wife, who was a keen horsewoman, explained: "I want to be ridden hard and put away wet." Unfortunately her husband had been asking: "What would you like me to do next?" This was not only a turn-off for her but made her wonder if her husband truly desired her. If this is your wife, she has probably been using code words— for example, "I want you to take the initiative more"—because she has been worried about damaging your sexual ego and your libido still further.

I have also counseled couples where the wife has not only been domineering but believed the myth that men are always up for sex (while in reality there are times when we are too tired, too stressed or have had too much to drink). These women have ended up pestering for sex, turning their husbands off and ending up feeling unattractive, rejected and angry.

What's the alternative?: Just like in verbal communication, good lovemaking is about being assertive. By this I mean being open and upfront about your desires (rather than sulking or having an affair) but also listening to your partner too, learning to talk about sex, negotiating how often and when, and compromising about what you each enjoy doing in bed and taking it in turns to set the agenda. (There is more advice in the next chapter and further reading at the end of the book.)

Drawing a line in the sand

By this point, you should have a clear idea about *why* your wife has stopped loving you. It might be something that she has complained about a million times before (but you have not really taken seriously until now), the build up of years of bad communication (that you have just diagnosed) or something that you have always known was a problem (but hoped would simply go away if you ignored it). In many cases, it is a combination of all three:

> *"I haven't made some of the best decisions when it comes to money and being a complete partner. Before we got married, I had to move to another city to complete my training and my wife quit her job to move with me. She couldn't find anything because the job market was horrible. She got pregnant and had an abortion. At the time, she didn't want to but I pressured her because of financial reasons. How-*

ever, I wasn't stepping up to the plate and being a real man. I should have taken care of her and the baby that she was going to give birth to. Thinking about it now, this decision had a huge emotional effect on her. I also complained about how bored I was living in this new city and was persuaded by my mother to return to my home town. My wife didn't want to go back because she felt we hadn't given this new city a chance and most importantly the cost of living was much cheaper. However, we didn't make the decision together as a couple, I let my mother influence me. To be honest, I feel like a coward but I have decided to try to become a better person. I'm going back to school and I'm attending counseling to restore my confidence and self-esteem. Is it possible for me to get my wife to love me again the way she used to?"

Whatever the circumstances behind your wife falling out of love, how do you stop the past mistakes from undermining your attempts to build a better future?

Making a fulsome apology

You have probably said you are sorry a million times before. Worse still, no matter how much you have promised that things will be different, your apology has fallen on deaf ears. So I would not be surprised if you're feeling a bit sceptical. However, I doubt that you've made a *fulsome* apology. What's the difference? Well "sorry" is just something that trips off our tongues, sometimes when we don't even mean it but want to keep the peace. Meanwhile, a fulsome apology has six key elements:

- *It acknowledges your unhelpful behavior*: For example, "I have not taken my share of responsibility for looking after the children."

- *It accepts your responsibility*: For example, "I was selfish and only thought about my own needs," or "I've hidden behind work pressures but there's been many times when I could have left earlier."

- *It identifies how this has made your partner feel*: For example, "It has left you feeling alone, frustrated and angry."

- *It expresses sorrow*: For example, "I'm really sorry for everything." You might even like to add a particular instance that you regret. "Most of all, I should have picked you up from the hospital after our son was born."

- *It explains why it won't happen again*: For example, "I'm going to try and leave earlier from work," or "I'm going to take our daughter to ice-skating competitions so I'm more involved in her hobbies." It is best to offer something specific—that can be measured or checked on—rather than something general (like trying harder) that could mean one thing to you and another to your wife.

- *It is sincere*: Choose a time when you're calm and collected, rather than angry, resentful or desperate—because that's how your apology will come across. Look your wife in the eye and check that your body language is open (no crossed legs or leaning away from her).

When I explain the fulsome apology lots of men insist, "but my wife already knows all that." On one level, they could be right but their wives still long to hear the words spoken out loud, because it truly acknowledges their feelings. As I've already explained, you can't acknowledge too often. Perhaps, in the past, you've also lessened the impact of an apology by adding a justification, or shared the blame around (for example, your mother or circumstances) and this has lessened your personal responsibility. In addition, you might have added a plea: "So why can't we try again?" It's a perfectly valid question but it is likely to put your wife's back up and raises the possibility that you're only saying this to win her back.

So think through your fulsome apology and write down something for every heading before you speak to your wife. Here is a recap:

- *Acknowledge unhelpful behavior*
- *Accept responsibility*
- *Identify how this made your partner feel*
- *Express sorrow*
- *Explain why it won't happen again*
- *Be sincere*

Finally, I cannot stress too strongly that you must be confident of delivering any changes rather than promising something unrealistic out of blind panic. For example, promising that you won't invite your mother to the house again, or that you'll find another job so you don't come into daily contact with the woman with whom you've been exchanging flirty texts is impractical and unrealistic. Could you really cast your mother out into the cold—however much she has undermined your wife—and what if you can't find any other suitable employment?

What if she doesn't respond or is just dismissive?

When you've made your fulsome apology, my advice is to give your wife a chance to reply but unless she is particularly keen to talk, walk away, making sure that you avoid tipping over into begging, pleading or other unhelpful behaviors that could undermine your good work. Anyway, it will probably take a while for everything you've said to her to sink in. And if you're the sort of man who plays his emotional cards close to his chest, she could be in shock! Whatever the response, please don't despair. You should see her softening over the next few days as she reflects on what you've said and when you've had a chance to deliver on your promises of different behavior.

Hopefully, your wife will accept your fulsome apology as this will draw a line in the sand between the past and the future, but if she doesn't, it will be because of one of the following reasons:

- She fears it will excuse your bad behavior.

- You might do it again.

- You don't deserve to be forgiven.

- She can only forgive if certain conditions are met.

Although it is helpful to explain that you're not looking to excuse your past behavior, I wouldn't get into a debate, reason with her or try to prove why she's wrong. Instead, I would use her scepticism to redouble your resolve to prove that you won't do it again, that you do deserve to be forgiven and that you will strive to meet any reasonable conditions for being forgiven.

Love Coach's Three Key Things to Remember:

- Most relationships deteriorate because of a variety of interlocking reasons.

- There is no one single magic bullet that will solve this crisis. However, better communication will lay the foundation for a better marriage.

- By apologizing for your mistakes, you will show your wife that you understand her unhappiness and commit to changing for the better.

Chapter Three

Can I fix things on my own?

"I have not been the best listener. I am a confrontational person who says what's on his mind and my wife is the opposite. She has kept all of her feelings about us bottled up until last month when it all came spilling out. She has told me that she needs to start living for herself, not me. She wants to grow as a person, and I am not the person she thinks can help her with that. There are a whole host of other issues, most of which can be summed up as communications related. We are currently still living together and sleeping in the same bed, but there is no intimacy. We have placed no timetable on when we might tell the kids, how we might tell the kids, and what a separation might look like. We are still spending the weekends together as a family at our ski house, and still have plans for a family vacation.

Our therapist has told me to give my wife psychic space, and to be patient. What else can I do? What can I or should I do to help this to a happy conclusion, which in my mind means keeping my family together?"

You've recovered from the shock of discovering your wife doesn't love you anymore, you've begun to understand why and you've made a fulsome apology. But how do you begin to fix things, especially if your wife is uncooperative or thinks it's too late? No wonder many men despair and ask me: "Doesn't it take two people to make a relationship?" So let me give you the good news. It might take two people to make things work in the long term but one person can get the ball rolling, initiate change and ultimately recruit the other to save the marriage. At this point, you're probably still feeling anxious and finding it hard to believe me. After all, you've been working your butt off and you've not only got little thanks to show for it but loads of hostility. So what's gone wrong? Unfortunately, the most common strategies for working on a relationship are fine under normal circumstances but these are not normal circumstances. At best, they will make your wife angry but, more likely and much worse, they may turn you into the enemy.

Five strategies that you think will work, but probably won't

I wouldn't be surprised if you've tried one or all of these strategies either because they've turned your relationship around in the past or it's what your family or friends have suggested. There is nothing wrong with any of these strategies, in moderation. Unfortunately, when they haven't worked, you've decided the problem was not trying hard enough rather than that the strategy was wrong. So guess what? You've pushed harder and harder and met more and more resistance. You've not only exhausted and depressed yourself but made your wife despair. So what are these five strategies that normally repair a relationship but are unlikely to work on yours?

Be Romantic

You've been telling her how attractive she looks, how much you appreciate her and you've arranged tickets to see her favorite band. In fact, you've been doing all those nice things she's always wanted but she *still* doesn't love you.

Why you think it will work: If someone doesn't try and lighten the mood, you will both become seriously depressed. What's more, you've seen the error of your ways and you want to start putting things right.

Why it doesn't work: Your wife will have noticed the changes and she will be torn in half. On one hand, she will want to smile at your jokes or soften to your loving gestures. On the other hand, she will fear that you can't keep these changes up and that, over time, everything will revert to normal and she'll be in the same situation again—only older. Don't forget, she's in terrible pain and she wants it to stop.

That's why the exit door seems very appealing but trying again seems only mildly tempting (because she can't risk getting her hopes up only to find herself back in the same place in 18 months' time). For some women, your gestures will be too little, too late or be seen as trying to buy her off—especially if your attempts to be romantic are getting bigger and bigger and turning manic.

Use the children

Of course you don't want her to be unhappy but there are some things that are more important than our own needs, like family and, most of all, children. In fact, she's being really selfish and shouldn't you point this out? If you have older children don't they have a right to know what's going on and have some say in the family's future?

Why you think it will work: She always says the children are her number one priority. So surely it would be best for them to be brought up by their mother *and* their father. You've read some research somewhere that children from broken homes do worse at school and are more likely to take drugs and end up in prison. So if she doesn't want to give you another chance, doesn't she owe it to the kids to at least try?

Why it doesn't work: Your wife doesn't need to be reminded how high the stakes are. She's probably been thinking of little else than how to protect the children. That's why she has been ignoring her unhappiness and in all honesty, they are the main reason why she didn't leave years ago! What's more, she's going to hear your concern for the kids as criticism of her as a mother. (This is not going to make her love you again!) She will be doubly angry if, in her eyes, you've often put *your* needs before those of the kids. The other problem with this strategy is that you will start frightening yourself: "Divorce will ruin my relationship with the kids," or "I'll never see my children again," or even, "My kids will call another man daddy." Such catastrophizing will *not* bring your wife to her senses but will make you panic and undo all your good work on saving your marriage. Finally, involving your children in your private disputes will widen any fault lines in your family and cause the long-term problems that you wish to avoid.

Have long talks

Since your wife has told you that she's no longer in love with you, the two of you have talked about little more than your situation, how she's feeling today, whether there's any hope and what can be done to change things.

Why you think it will work: Everybody knows that you can't solve a problem without sitting down and talking about it. Certainly ignoring the problem isn't going to make it go away. And wasn't that how you got into this mess in the first place?

Why it doesn't work: Good communication is at the heart of a good marriage but going around in circles isn't good communication. Constantly asking her about her feelings and whether any of your efforts have changed anything is like digging up a seed to see if it has germinated! Worse still, these long talks just suck any remaining fun and spontaneity out of your marriage. No wonder she wants to leave! Anything for a quiet life.

Try to be intimate

When she isn't sitting at the opposite end of the living room, you've been giving her back rubs or massaging her feet. In bed, you've been stroking her hair because you know she really likes that.

Why you think it will work: A touch is worth a thousand words and you're desperate to show just how much you love her. Even though she seldom, if ever, returns that favor, just being allowed to be close to her makes you feel that all is not lost.

Why it doesn't work: There is a big danger that you will come across as terribly needy—which is not very appealing. If she turns away, you will probably react like a little boy whose ice cream has fallen onto the pavement and that's going to make her feel cruel and heartless or angry because she feels you're putting pressure on her. There is also an elephant in the room: SEX. Many couples who have found themselves at "I love you but . . ." have fallen into the all-or-nothing trap where any kissing or cuddling (beyond a brief peck hello and goodbye) tends to turn into full intercourse. So, in her mind's eye, you're not trying to be intimate but angling for make-up sex.

Suppress your issues with the relationship

You've been doing your best to keep everything nice. Even if she's bitten your head off—perhaps because you were late getting home and helping out with the children—you've tried to smile sweetly but said nothing. On a bigger scale, while she's gone on at length about what needs to be different (if there is to be any chance of salvaging anything), you've kept quiet about what's been making you unhappy. After all, you will do *anything* to save your relationship.

Why you think it will work: She's got enough issues to keep an army of counselors busy for the next 20 years, so you don't want to add yours to the pile. And won't it just confirm her fears that your marriage is past saving?

Why it doesn't work: Walking on eggshells just makes your wife irritated or snappy. When you back down—even in the face of unreasonable behavior—she loses all respect. Worse still, she knows you're repressing stuff (which puts her on edge as she's not certain whether it's about helping out with the kids or something bigger) and you don't come across as "real." On a deeper level, she knows that you will not do *anything* to save your relationship. For example, you won't agree to live in a sexless marriage or allow her to take another lover! In effect, she can't reason with "I'll do anything"—because instead of a sensible dialogue you're hiding behind this blanket statement. By contrast, if there are things that *you* want to change too, it shows you have a real stake in changing your marriage for the better—rather than simply appeasing your wife.

Five strategies that probably will work

I hope that you're beginning to understand what's gone wrong, feeling a little more optimistic and ready to roll up your sleeves. Good. It's time to lay the foundations for winning back your wife.

Don't wait to recruit your wife

Instead of waiting for your wife to agree that your marriage can be saved or for her not to be so negative or to give you some encouragement, this strategy imagines that she is 100 percent on board. For a minute, imagine the relief and the joy. Your heart will have stopped racing and a huge weight will have been lifted off your shoulders. However, if you are honest, you'll also be aware that this is only the beginning of the journey. A lot of work still needs be done to turn this relationship around. Think for a second: what would you like to change about your behavior? Write down these goals as this will underline your determination to follow them through. For example: "I'm going to do more about the house," and "I'm going to listen to what she says, truly listen," and "I'm going to be more positive and leave work pressures at work." Now you must act as if your wife is committed to saving your marriage and start putting your plan into action.

Why this will work: Time and again, couples get stuck because both are waiting for a sign from the other (so they can change) or reassurance (so they don't risk getting hurt) but that leaves each partner in a very passive position—waiting for their other half. However, imagining that your wife is on board or has shown that she has feelings frees you from this trap and allows you to get to work.

Take the pressure off

If your ways of working on saving your relationship have simply pushed your wife away or, as she sees it, put her under pressure, then it is time to acknowledge everything you regret and identify the impact of your behavior on her. For example: "I know that I have been trying to make you feel guilty and that's just made you angry," or "I've been wearing you down with constant questions and that's made you exasperated." Next, and most importantly, make a commitment to stop. For example: "I'm no longer going to beg," or "I accept that you don't know why you've fallen out of love." Finally, explain your commitment to change and lay out your manifesto: "Although I'm no longer going to... (for example: 'ask for a second chance') that doesn't mean that I don't think we can sort this out. However, I'm aware that pressuring you doesn't work. Instead of just talking about change, I'm going to show you how much I can change (or how things could be different). In the meantime, I'm not going to instigate further conversations about us but that doesn't mean I'm not up for one if you'd like to talk in the future."

Why this will work: Taking the pressure off will not only improve the atmosphere in the house but allow things to return to something more normal. What's more, by explaining your behavior, your intentions and inviting further conversations (on her terms) you have taken an important step to more open and honest communication.

Flip/flop your default behaviour

When you're stressed and anxious, you tend to respond in the same old way. For example, you get angry, go silent or avoid confrontation. Although, you know your default reaction doesn't work—because you've tried it a million times before—you can't stop yourself from doing it yet again. Perhaps, you hope that by reacting bigger (shouting louder, sulking longer or getting down on your knees) or reacting in the same old way one more time, it will change the situation. Maybe, you're not sure how else to react. That's the beauty of the flip/flop strategy: you flip over your old failed flop behaviour. Ultimately, it doesn't matter how you act differently because anything is better than the same old, same old (as you know where that leads). So why not try doing the opposite? If you get angry, try being calm. If you clam up, try explaining how you're feeling. If you avoid confrontation, look at the section on assertiveness.

Why this will work: By breaking out of old habits, you will have opened up the possibility of a different outcome. Even if your alternative approach doesn't work, it has shown your wife that you can change and this provides hope for the future.

Learn to speak her love language

There are five ways of showing how much you love your wife. These are: "Caring Actions" (for example, picking up her dry cleaning); "Affectionate Physical Contact" (for example, stroking the back of her neck while you watch TV together); "Appreciative Words" (for example, "Thank you for coming with me when I took my mother to the doctor's office"); "Creating Quality Time Together" (for example, taking her out for a meal) or "Present Giving" (for example, "I picked up these flowers because I was thinking about you."). Unfortunately, we tend to express our love in the way that we'd like to receive it. So you might be showering her with appreciative words—because that's what you need right now—but she doesn't really hear your love because her love language is caring actions.

Why this will work: It will target your energy into the love language that is most effective to winning back your wife, so you're not worn out, resentful and wondering why nothing you do or say makes any difference.

Model the behavior that you'd like to see from her

When you're hurt or upset, it is very easy to take your frustration out on your wife. You justify it to yourself because, "what can she expect if she does . . ." or "if she hadn't done x, I wouldn't have done y." Unfortunately, your "bad" behavior will spark something equally unpleasant from your wife and before long, you're caught in a negative spiral—matching each other dig for dig in a race to the bottom. However, there is an alternative. If you've got children, do you ever ask them to be the "big one"; to put aside their hurt and make peace when they fall out with their friends? In this way, one kind or conciliatory gesture sparks another one and before too long, you have a positive upward spiral. So why not try being calm and pleasant and give your wife the benefit of the doubt? For example, if she comes home late without phoning, think that it is because she was really enjoying being out with her friends rather than dreading coming home to you. The first interpretation would make you warm and welcoming and the second cold and angry.

Why this will work: This is a concrete way to take responsibility and kick start change in your relationship. More important, it will encourage your wife to be generous as well and start to give you the benefit of the doubt too.

How being assertive can turn around your relationship

I'm now going to unveil the big gun that's going to save your marriage. However, it won't come as a huge surprise because I've highlighted it time and time again. Whatever the reasons why your wife has fallen out of love and whatever mistakes you've made trying to win her back, the key to transforming your relationship is improving day-to-day communication.

"My wife started making the bed, making sure she was sighing loud enough so I could hear. Apparently I should have done it myself, or at least be helping. I told her that I had been washing the dishes and that she could have called me for help. She replied that she doesn't have to tell me everything, that I should know things. Ten minutes afterward I remembered a watch I had bought her, so I went to get it. She had dropped it to the floor, and it seemed like it stopped working. She asked me, 'What now, what do we do about the watch?' I replied, 'We should take it to a store to see if it's broken.' She said all stores were closed and asked again what should we do. I said that in that case, I didn't know. Perhaps wait for Monday? That's when she replied that I never helped her with anything. Similar episodes corroded the whole day, and by the evening, I couldn't take it anymore and burst into tears (if I recall it properly, for I was so mad with rage and helplessness) and I told her that I am so tired of trying so hard to get things right with us and always feeling alone . . ."

Although good communication is the big gun for winning back your wife, no opportunity is too small for you to practice being different. In fact, everyday squabbles are the best place to start as the stakes are much smaller. I would sum up the best approach in two words: Be Assertive.

The Assertiveness Rights

Instead of your wants, needs or beliefs or those of your partner taking precedence, with assertiveness, you both have equal rights:

1. To hold and express your own opinions.

2. To refuse requests without feeling guilty.

3. To set your own priorities and goals.

4. To judge your own behavior, thoughts and emotions.

5. To take responsibility for the consequences.

So how does this work in practice? Assertiveness is all about being open and honest (rather than hiding your feelings) but it also respects the other person (and takes account of what it might be like to hear your message). With this in mind, I would suggest the following:

- *Think ahead.* Be clear about what you are trying to achieve.

- *Say something positive about your partner or the situation.* For example: "I know you have been trying hard," or "We seem to have been getting on much better."

- *Be specific and direct.* For example: "I would like us to share the bed together again," rather going for global goals such as, "I would like you to be more affectionate," which are hard to measure and could mean something different to your wife than they do for you. For example, she might think you mean intercourse when you actually mean a kiss hello or goodbye.

- *Choose your timing.* Don't wait until your partner is about to go out the door but conversely don't bottle up your feelings until they explode out (as tears or anger).

- *Check your body language.* Look your wife in the eye. Aim for an upright and relaxed posture with your arms by your side (rather than crossed).

- *Avoid unassertive words.* For example: "I wonder if . . ." or "Could it be possible that..."

- *Stick to the facts and avoid the judgments.* For example: "I find it hard to sleep in the spare room," or "The sofa is bad for my back," rather than, "It makes me feel so unwanted."

- *Anticipate possible objections.* Be aware of how your wife might answer (for example: "It will put me under pressure") but don't try and head off objections (for example: "I know you don't want me to come back to the bed because that would not be giving you space"), as this will weaken your request.

- *Be prepared to negotiate.* Remember that your wife has the right to say no. However, if she doesn't explain why, then you should ask about her reservations rather than backing down right away. Perhaps if you had a greater understanding of her position, you could change your request to something that she could accept. For example, if she doesn't want you to return to the bedroom—as this might give the wrong signals—you could agree to not trying to initiate sex for the time being.

Returning to the last case history letter, here is an example of how better communication and learning to be more assertive can turn a difficult situation around:

"My wife started crying, said she was so sorry about upsetting me and that she didn't want to make me suffer anymore. That we should end it all. That she couldn't give me what I wanted, that she didn't see me as a lover anymore but as a friend. After a short period of recovering from the shock (those words always strike you as a novelty, even though I've heard them before), I went for a night walk to clear my mind and decided to be assertive and confront the problem. As soon as I arrived home, I asked what was it about me that got on her nerves. She looked at me with a bored expression, 'Here we go again. You and your conversations that lead nowhere. Can we please not talk about it? I'm tired of talking. It seems that all we do is talk.' Then I remembered 'the five languages of love' and how 'Caring Actions' was the number one language for her. I related that with her father never helping her mother at home, and how that made for an

unhappy household. I told her that probably she's afraid that I will turn out to be like her father, and that's why she was always picking on me about never helping at home. She confessed that there was truth in that."

If your wife is domineering

I'm not going to pretend it is easy to communicate with an aggressive, angry or domineering woman, especially if she is more articulate and better at arguing than you. However, your previous strategy of appeasing, "yes dear" or being passive aggressive, "I meant to do it, honest" or simply keeping your head down has not worked and brought you to this crisis point. So how do you become more assertive?

Stand your ground

I'm not suggesting picking a fight but next time you feel unfairly criticized you should stand up for yourself. Remember that you have just as much right to your opinion as she does to hers. Make it something small and specific and act right away. For example, she asks you to select a wine in a restaurant and then complains about your choice. Tell her why you chose that wine: "You liked it last time we had it," rather than inwardly fuming. Maybe, she complains that your son did not have a bedtime story when she went out for the evening and left you in charge. Tell her your thinking: "We did a jigsaw together instead to wind down and get ready to sleep." Remember there is more than one way of putting a child to bed and yours is equally valid.

Why it works: It makes your wife stop, think and be aware of how her behavior impacts on other people. Speaking up also brings all the conflict out into the open where it can be dealt with. Many wives complain that their husbands won't argue, which drives them mad. So although she might be annoyed at being challenged at the time, she could be pleased later. Better still, you have chosen the battleground (where you have a strong case) rather than being ambushed (where you probably won't).

Acknowledge her anger

You won't be surprised by this next strategy as it fits into my theme of acknowledge, acknowledge and acknowledge again. Rather than trying to distract: "Would you like a cup of tea?" or rationalize away her anger: "I know the kids have been difficult," or solve her problem on the spot: "Why don't I go out and come in again," just listen and acknowledge: "So you're feeling angry . . ." Follow up with questions: "Why has this made you so angry?" and "How could we do things differently?"

Why it works: Although you will probably get another blast of anger: "Of course I'm really angry because you can't do the simplest thing"; when a feeling is expressed it will burn itself out. It's only when it is pushed underground or converted into toxic thoughts such as "he doesn't care," that they solidify into a concrete wall around your wife's heart. By staying with her feelings, rather than physically or emotionally running away, you will find out what's behind the anger (and it might be something different from what you assumed) and she will feel heard. Even better, by acknowledging her feelings, you are a step away from acknowledging your own and standing up for yourself.

Help her feel emotionally safe

Instead of letting your wife spiral out of control, so one issue leads to another and then another or her feelings build from mild irritation to total fury, I'd like you to help her feel safe. We've already covered one of the best ways: acknowledging her feelings. You could also ask her what's wrong—rather than letting her build up a head of steam. Think of it as letting off a pressure valve. Sometimes humor will work, or touch (everything from a light touch on the shoulder to a hug). If she is talking up a storm and raising a hundred points but not letting you get a word in edgewise, I want you to interrupt her. I know this is not going to be popular but don't dismiss the idea just yet. Tell her: "I can't deal with five issues at the same time," or: "Could I just respond to what you're saying?" If she demands to finish, let her and then tell her: "You want me to speak more/take more initiative/tell you what I'm thinking, but you keep cutting me off/don't give me a chance/or don't listen properly." Remember, you have an equal right to be heard and that includes equal time to argue your case (or at least to respond to hers).

Why it works: Although it is horrible being on the receiving end of a whirlwind of emotions, it is just as tough at the eye of the storm. Think of being like the Tasmanian Devil cartoon character with eyes, legs and arms spinning in all directions. It must be truly frightening. You never know what's going to happen, what you're going to say or what damage you're going to do. By contrast, if someone helps you feel safe—either physically with a hug, or emotionally by acknowledging your feelings and breaking the issues down into manageable chunks —you are going to feel much, much calmer. You will also feel loved and cared for too.

Criticize her behavior, not her personality

In many ways, this strategy is another way of containing the situation as you are complaining about something your wife has done rather than about her as a person. While she is probably likely to accept, for example, that criticizing you in front of the children is unfair, telling her that she is thoughtless or a bad mother is going to be like throwing a lighted match onto petrol.

Why it works: Criticizing a particular behavior—preferably just after it has happened—keeps the argument about one specific incident, which should be reasonably easy to resolve. By contrast, talking about her personality invites her to defend herself: either by listing all the incidents when she was not thoughtless or, more likely, going on the attack and pointing out all your failings.

Broken record technique

If your wife steamrollers over you, refuses to listen, changes the subject or dismisses your point of view, repeat it and maybe repeat it again. Imagine a broken record where a needle gets stuck or a dirty CD where the same piece of information is repeated over and over again. This is a very powerful intervention and should be used sparingly for really important issues.

Why it works: Not only does it stop you from becoming sidetracked, but it also keeps you in the argument for that crucial bit longer. Time and again, in my counseling room, couples resolve issues—rather than one partner just backing down—because I encourage the quieter and less assertive partner to stand firm. If this strategy sounds rude, it can be softened by alternating the acknowledgment of your wife's opinion or feelings with repeating your point.

Don't push things under the carpet

What drives your wife's anger more than anything else is feeling that she is not being truly heard. So the worst thing you can say is: "How can we avoid this problem?" or "Calm down," as this will seem like you are denying her feelings or you are not interested. Unfortunately, she is probably right—you *are* uncomfortable with her negative feelings and have, in the past, tried to push them under the carpet. So be aware that even mild strategies to calm her—like changing the subject or making a joke—could be heard as ignoring her feelings. Your wife has been so programmed to expect: "Please take those nasty feelings away," or "I can't cope when you're like this," and is either unaware or unconvinced of your desire to change, that she could hear a denial of her emotions—even when one isn't meant. So how do you get round this problem? Yes, you've guessed it! Acknowledge, acknowledge, acknowledge: "I can see you're angry," or "Why are you angry?" or "I'd like to understand but I'd find it easier to take everything on board if we took things one by one." Be aware without using acknowledging as one of your calming strategies—probably at the rate of three acknowledges to one other—it could be heard as pushing things under the carpet.

Why it works: If you ignore your wife's upset, it will seem to her that you are denying her feelings and, to a woman, that feels like you are denying her. Remember, your goal is to help your wife switch back on her feelings and that means letting out all the negative ones too. Don't worry though, the positive ones—love, respect, desire—will follow on behind. Better still, if you can accept her darker emotions (as well as the lighter ones) she will feel that you can accept the real her.

If your wife is passive

In many ways, it is easier to turn around your relationship when your wife is not about to bite your head off—although she is probably still angry but in a passive way. (So please read the previous section too.) Most wives who put the kids' and their husband's needs before their own find it hard to stand up for what they truly want and to be assertive. At this point, you're probably going to shrug or worse still start to despair: "How can I teach my wife to be assertive? Especially as she thinks the relationship is doomed and is not going to want to read some book." Please don't panic. You're only responsible for your half of communication.

However, if you change and become assertive (rather than domineering) this will have a positive effect on how your wife communicates. Basically, I'm going to show you how to improve your listening skills and this will help her be more forthcoming.

Draw her out

Nod your head encouragingly, repeat back the last thing she has said and ask questions. Anything that will give her time to think and delve deeper into how she feels.

Why this works: From when she was a little girl, your wife has been trained to think of others or not be pushy and therefore she will not automatically consider her own needs.

Double Check

Instead of just assuming that she is on board with a plan, check and check again: "Are you sure you want to have a picnic?" or "Wouldn't you rather do something else?" This is especially important when she seems to be in a bad mood for no apparent reason.

Why this works: Instead of taking her silence or some half-hearted interest in a project as agreement, she has a second opportunity to tell you what's really on her mind.

Look at her body language

Are your wife's shoulders slumped, her eyes downcast and lips pouted? Does she have her arms crossed or her back to you? Is she talking so quietly that you can hardly hear? These are all signs that she feels unfairly treated, downtrodden or is having trouble standing up for herself. So ask her: "What does that sigh mean?" or "Why did you just shrug your shoulders?"

Why this works: When there is a mismatch between what her lips say: "I'm fine," or "Don't worry about me" and what her body language is telling you, it's normally a sign that she's really struggling to be assertive.

Give her permission to say no

Sometimes people need support to say no. So tell her you won't be upset if she disagrees or wants to do something else: "It's not that important, so if you'd rather not," or "I'd prefer you to tell me what you're really thinking," or just "Are you sure?'

Why this works: If your wife is a people pleaser, she's going to worry that you'll think less of her or that she will let people down and therefore not be a "good person." This strategy offers reassurance that you would rather have the truth than too easy agreement.

Give her notice

Bring up contentious issues as early as possible, so your wife has a chance to think through all the angles. For example, if you're going to have to travel for work, don't tell her at the last minute (when there are fewer options) but raise it as soon as you know it might be happening.

Why this works: It forces you to be assertive too, rather than sneaking unwelcome news past her at the last minute and offers both of you time to talk through all the angles, negotiate and find a solution that works for both of you.

Praise her

I'm not talking about telling her she looks nice or is a good cook—not that there's anything wrong with such compliments—but something specifically targeted at any assertive behavior. For example: "Thank you for telling me that you were unhappy about me going away for the weekend. I really enjoyed staying here and being with you," or "It really helped knowing you were angry as I went away and had a long think about it."

Why this works: We all need positive feedback and this strategy reinforces change and makes it easier for your wife to be assertive in the future.

Sex and winning back your wife

If pushing for intimacy risks pushing your wife away, then what do you do with all your tender feelings and your desire to show her that your sex life could be so much more rewarding?

> *"My wife told me 'I don't love you' after I pushed why we could not get close anymore. We had drifted apart after our second child who is now four. Our eldest is five. Our sex life went downhill at that point (she also has a prolapse) and we have not been good at keeping our marriage close (work and kids and split lives). She tells me she is not happy but does not believe we can fix this. We both want a close relationship leading to something physical but she can't see this happening with me. She says there is no one else. I can't believe I didn't deal with this earlier. I assumed that things would work out as the boys got older. What can I do or is the writing on the wall?"*

Acknowledge where you are

Instead of hoping sexual relations will improve at some unspecified point in the future, it is time to face not only your wife's disappointment but your own too. If there are any underlying medical problems, speak to your doctor. I can't tell you how often I see women who've put up with painful intercourse due to a gynecological problem without getting help and men who've suffered with erectile dysfunction without looking into the causes. I know it might seem rather academic if you're not having sex at the moment anyway but talking about problems (and agreeing to seek help) is solid proof that you want to change. Other contentious issues that need acknowledging include: pornography, poor body image and personal inhibitions. If you have young children and your wife has no sexual desire, please be reassured—especially if you have two kids under five. It takes the hormones in a woman's body about 18 months to return to normal after childbirth but this is the point when many women get pregnant again. However, rest assured, although your wife will not feel spontaneously turned on, she can still be sexually responsive and become turned on.

Put a ban on sex

Couples often laugh when I suggest agreeing to ban sex because many haven't been intimate for months on end. However, there is a big difference between something happening by accident and making a conscious agreement. By ruling out sex—by which I mean intercourse, oral sex, shared masturbation and playing with your wife's breasts—you can free yourself up to enjoy other forms of physical intimacy (like kissing, cuddling and stroking) without your wife worrying that you're angling for sex or you worrying whether you will be successful this time.

Enjoy stress-free intimacy

It's a bit like being a teenager again. Remember when you couldn't go "all the way" and how much you enjoyed heavy petting and the pleasure of being able to hold a real woman; how she smelled and the taste of her lipstick? Instead of rushing to the main pleasure spots, enjoy lying together and being sensual rather than sexual together. When you're both feeling relaxed, start to explore the rest of each other's bodies (beyond breasts, vagina and penis). Although you might fear this is going to be a bit tame—in comparison with the relief of an orgasm—cuddling can be just as intimate and in many ways more intimate than just rubbing sexual parts together. It will also make your wife feel loved rather than just a sex object.

Do more around the house

It might seem strange to put household chores and child care into a section about sex but all the research shows a clear link between how much a man does around the house and the quality and frequency of a couple's love life (and how likely they are to get divorced too). So why should this be? Modern marriage is supposed to be equal with everything split down the middle. Although most men sign up to this idea in principle, it is easy to find lots of reasons why a chore doesn't need to be done now. Meanwhile, women step into the gap between intention and execution. Before too long, they are running the house, cleaning the bathroom and remembering to buy toilet paper while men are "helping out". It's the same with bringing up children: once again, most new parents want to take an equal role but breastfeeding a clingy baby or demands at work will leave most women doing the lion's share—even when a couple are out together. The other day on the train, I saw a man in a suit taking his toddler daughter, who was also dressed up for a special occasion, off to the toilet. It was great to watch a man with such an easy and loving relationship with his child but it wasn't this that made them stick in my mind. When he returned to his seat, I saw that his wife was there too—looking out of the window. She was wearing a smart outfit too and they must have been going off to a wedding, graduation ceremony or some formal event. What made this family stand out was that the man was in charge of both looking after and entertaining their child while his wife relaxed and just enjoyed the journey.

If a woman is doing more than her fair share of chores and childcare, she is not only tired—with sex dropping further down her "to do" list—but resentful and that's a complete passion killer. She might not necessarily put it like this but deep down she's thinking, "why should I have sex with him when he obviously thinks so little about me?" The whole situation is worse if she feels you will only do something when you're asked or with bad grace.

So although, you might not have thought of it like this, if you empty the laundry basket or clean the kitchen after you've cooked or take the children off her hands, you will increase your chance of sex (or a loving gesture if the situation between you is really grim) because your wife will see this as being attentive and loving.

Love Coach's Three Key Things
to Remember:

- Relationships are turned around by facing and solving small everyday issues.

- Don't swallow your needs, wants and opinions and don't pressure your wife to do the same either.

- Avoid focusing on your wife's genitals and breasts so you don't make her feel that you just want sex rather than to make love to all of her.

Chapter Four

How can I keep strong when I'm getting no encouragement from my wife?

"I've been implementing change, showing my wife affection, doing more around the house, rubbing her shoulders, chasing her around for sex—she is fairly receptive when she's not tired from baby duties. I've also made a point of starting to watch more TV shows with her after the baby is asleep, suggesting we do things together on the weekend, getting involved in things that she has an interest in, etc. However, she still does not 'repay' the favor and is generally cold—not icy—but enough to know that something still is not right. I guess I'm just feeling

that she isn't putting in really any effort to our rela-
tionship, like she is on autopilot until she can leave.
I love her dearly and don't want to break up our
family unit. Is there any hope?"

Change is difficult, especially when you're not getting any encouragement or feedback from your wife. Worse still, she could be cold, angry or dismissive. At this point, it is very easy to become disheartened and to forget the progress that you've made. So let's recap on what you've achieved and how it has changed the situation. First, you have apologised for past mistakes. Second, you have recognized the strategies that you thought were helping save your marriage but were pushing her further away, and stopped them. Third, you have started to listen—really listen—and have a better idea of what needs to change long term for your relationship to thrive. Now you are ready for the next phase of your fight back: *Implementing change*.

The well-made plan

It is fine to have an overall goal, for example saving your marriage. However, when faced by hostility or, perhaps even worse, apathy, it is easy to be blown off course, start to despair and give up hope. In contrast, if you have a detailed plan with lots of smaller goals, you are less likely to lose your way or be discouraged. So how can you test whether you have a well-made plan? Ask yourself if it is SMART:

Specific

Measurable

Achievable

Realistic

Timed (i.e., there is a date for completion)

For example, a *specific* goal might be spending 10 minutes talking about each other's day. This goal is also *measurable* because you can look back at the end of the week and check how often you talked. If your wife is sullen and refuses to engage, it might not be *achievable*. If you secretly expect one small change alone to achieve a breakthrough, your plan is not particularly *realistic* (although as part of a larger portfolio of changes, it might make a significant contribution). Finally, if your plan is, for example, to lay the new patio that she's always wanted, but your work is so demanding at the moment that you won't be able to get around to it for a while, it is not *timed*.

Finding structure and focus

Most men lose hope because they are rushing around in circles—trying everything and anything to make things better—rather than being focused on SMART changes. So here are five key questions to ask yourself:

What is my goal? I would like you to have around three intermediate goals to support your main goal (saving your marriage or getting your wife to fall back in love). They could be something about improving communication or becoming a better listener or sharing your feelings more. They could be something practical like taking over the laundry or switching your phone off after seven pm or bathing the children three nights a week. They could be something fun like going away for the weekend or taking the children to the park on Sunday afternoons. If you are unclear what your wife might appreciate, think back to what she has always complained about but, in the past, you have discounted or ignored.

What are my resources? By this I mean, what personal qualities will help you reach this goal? It could be, for example, your love for your wife, the support of your mother (who will babysit) or this book. It might be money, determination, "I never give up without a fight," or 20 years of marriage. At times like this, it is easy to overlook just how much you have going for you.

What are my obstacles? This question is aimed at predicting possible problems. Obstacles can be personal, for example: "I can be lazy," or "Once I sit down, I never get up and help," or "I tend to turn a small setback into a major catastrophe." They can also be about your circumstances, "I have a demanding job," or "I'm worried about the health of my father."

What changes do I need to make? Think about your obstacles and what you might need to do to overcome them. For example, you could aim to leave earlier from work or not allow yourself to sit down and relax with a beer until after eight pm. Try to come up with changes that are SMART.

What would support these changes? This is about making small changes that will help turn your intermediate goals into a reality. For example, starting to delegate more at work or listening to a relaxation CD in the car to unwind on the way home.

For each of your intermediate goals, go through all the questions and write down a few key prompts to provide structure and focus for the week ahead. For example: "I am going to listen to my wife more and therefore I will let her finish what she's saying without interrupting. If I feel tempted, I will actually bite the end of my tongue." From time to time, go back and refresh your intermediate goals.

What if my wife is still not noticing my efforts?

You wouldn't be human if you didn't sometimes feel overwhelmed by negative thoughts or feel down and depressed.

> *"What is killing me right now is that there is no significant improvement in 'us.' We are in stasis and the longer it lasts the less certain I feel that we will survive and the more I feel that something stupid will happen, i.e. one of us walking out. I hate that. I want to regain a love that endures and grows, but at times my wife is so very cold. Sometimes she doesn't want to talk about us and I find the lack of knowledge about what is happening hard to deal with. I want her to be attracted to me again; I can't believe she feels that way about me now, it's such a shock.*

> *I'm trying to be patient and instigate change, now I*
> *know what I've done wrong, but feel the sands of*
> *time working against us. I love her so much."*

Fortunately, these sorts of doubts and anxieties can be useful. However, there is a difference between using setbacks and blocks in a constructive manner and letting them undermine you. So what's the difference?

Five worst things to do if you're losing faith

Coming back from "I don't love you anymore" is a long and arduous journey, so perhaps it's not surprising that you might be tempted by a few coping strategies that might take the edge off your pain but actually makes things worse.

Push for an answer

When you're going through a tough time, one of the main ways of coping is to look for light at the end of the tunnel. No wonder you're after reassurance that your wife will keep an open mind or that you keep trying to make her agree that staying together is the preferred goal. At your lowest moments, you would rather have a decision—even if it's not the outcome you want—rather than bear the uncertainty anymore.

Why this doesn't work: The only answer that she can give, at the moment, is that she is unhappy, doesn't know what she wants or that you should call it a day. It might give you a burst of relief that you know the answer but five minutes later, you will be begging her to think again. By contrast, uncertainty is your friend. It buys you time to work on your relationship.

Self-medicate

Your head is so full of plans, trying to second-guess what will make her happy and full of anxiety about how she will react, that you need to switch off from time to time or go completely mad. So what's the harm in getting drunk, watching Internet porn, gambling, taking recreational drugs or anything else that will give you a break from your over-active mind? Alternatively, you might boost your self-confidence by signing up to an online dating site or flirting with a stranger in a chat room.

Why this doesn't work: I can't tell you how often men ruin their chances of winning back their wives by retreating into the sort of destructive behaviors that made her fall out of love in the first place. The odds are that she will find out about your Internet habits and take you through what seemed like harmless fun in excruciating detail.

Act out

Just because you are trying not to be angry with your wife, doesn't mean that the feelings will disappear. Instead, they will burst out somewhere that they don't belong. I have known men who have picked a fight at work (and triggered disciplinary procedures) or been snappy with their children (and created a bad atmosphere at home).

Why this doesn't work: Not only will you be a bear with a sore head—which is hardly going to make you more loveable—but you risk convincing your wife that your reaction is not just transitory (due to extraordinary circumstances) but part of your character (and therefore permanent). As it is impossible never to be angry, it is better to *report* your feelings: "I feel angry when you turn away when I'm talking," rather than acting them out by slamming doors, snide comments or muttering under your breath.

Let other people talk you down

You're feeling miserable so it seems sensible to offload to friends, family and anybody else who will listen. Unfortunately, because these people love you, they want you to feel better. Often they are uncomfortable with the extremes of despair that accompany coping with your wife falling out of love so it is no surprise that they suggest accepting the inevitable or throwing in the towel.

Why this doesn't work: Your friends and family can't see the bigger picture, especially when they are confronted by your pain, and they are not sure what you want from them. Next time you need to offload, explain that you're looking for a chance to talk, some sympathy and lots of support but there is no need to give advice. Ultimately, you know what is best for you.

Ignore the problems

If your wife is cold or snappy, it is tempting to walk away and wait until she is in a better mood. Similarly, when the atmosphere in the house drops below freezing point, you decide to spend more time at work or hide behind your laptop. Alternatively, you will give yourself a pep talk and rationalize away your fears.

Why this doesn't work: If you're feeling depressed or anxious, there could be a good reason. Perhaps you've been making some stupid mistakes and need to up your game. Perhaps your wife is being negative because you've made the wrong diagnosis of the underlying problems, or you're heading in the right direction but pushing too far too fast. Whatever the situation, treat your feelings as your allies; listen to them and see what they have to tell you. In this way, something that seems destructive—her negative feelings—can be turned into something constructive.

Five best things to do when you're losing faith

Even if you're making all the right moves—listening to your wife, acknowledging her feelings and making SMART changes —there will be times when you're tired, stressed and down. So here are five ways to keep sane when the going gets tough.

Cut yourself some slack

Change is difficult and it takes time to replace unhelpful habits with helpful ones. I never worry about setbacks unless people don't learn anything from them.

Why this works: Instead of running yourself down, and getting depressed and demotivated, you can look back over what went wrong and fine-tune your plan. So be kind to yourself: you are going through one of the biggest challenges that a man can face and you're doing OK.

Live in the moment

Instead of worrying about past mistakes or being anxious about the future, focus on making it through today and the next seven days. What are the possible pitfalls over the weekend? When are you likely to feel down? What could head off those problems? If you find yourself thinking further into the future, bring your focus back to today and tomorrow.

Why this works: Although we spend a lot of time thinking about the past or planning the future, we can only live in the present. So whenever you find yourself worrying about some distant tomorrow, tell yourself: "This is the age of uncertainty. I can't change the past and I can't know the future but I can make today better."

Put yourself in your wife's shoes

When you're upset, it is easy to focus on *what* your wife has done rather than *why*. So instead of listing all the hurtful things, step back and try and understand what is driving her behavior. Time and again, people behave badly because they are frightened. So ask yourself: "Why is my wife so fearful?" You most probably know the answer already. She is frightened of letting down her defenses and getting hurt again. She is frightened that she might stay but find herself in the same place five years down the line. She is frightened that you can't or won't change.

Why this works: Imagine that your wife is holed up in a castle with a moat and a drawbridge. Instead of trying to blast or starve her out, I'd like you to light a fire and start roasting something delicious. Putting yourself into her shoes will help you understand, be kind and compassionate and this, in turn, will encourage her to put aside her fears and lower the drawbridge.

Go to a good place

If your thinking has tipped over from helpful reflection into obsessing, a good strategy is to imagine yourself in a good place. This can be somewhere that you have always enjoyed or felt safe (perhaps a holiday cottage from your childhood or sitting on your grandmother's lap) or somewhere in your imagination (a deserted beach with crickets singing in the dunes). Alternatively, you could put yourself into a good place by doing an activity that is engrossing and calming. For example, going for a run, meditating, doing a crossword or tinkering with the car.

Why this works: While self-medicating tries to block out the feelings, going to a good place is merely a temporary distraction. While self-medicating turns off your brain, going to a good place allows it to keep working in the background. Often when you're engrossed in something all consuming and least expecting it, an answer or a useful insight will pop into your mind.

Read this book again

Instead of relying on your team of friends and supporters, the answer might be in this book (or another one of my books or one from another author). Reading is a good way of stepping back and getting a new insight.

Why this works: Good books have many ideas and countless pieces of wisdom. It is not so much that you can't absorb everything at the first sitting but different things will strike you at different places on your journey. This is especially important if you tend to wolf down self-help books for the comfort and hope that they offer. Although you will take away the main message—for example, you can win back your wife—it is only when you return and read slowly that you can start to learn and grow.

I never really loved you

Sometimes it is hard to keep faith because the message from your wife is so overwhelmingly negative that it makes you lose all hope:

"My wife and I have been married for 18 years. We have two children together. After feeling distant from her over the course of the last year and half, I asked her a simple question a couple nights ago, 'Do you still like me?' The bombshell, of course, was her reply: 'I love you, but I am not romantically in love with you.' She explained that she wants to be happy, personally. Matter of fact, she said that she has not loved me romantically over these entire 18 years. I didn't understand what she meant by 'romantic love,' so I asked her, but she had difficulty defining it. I've the same problem with 'personal happiness.' I know it sounds stupid, but she desires this more than repairing our relationship, it seems. How do we discuss this love, if we are at a loss for words? So I ordered your book: I Love You, But I'm Not in Love With You, but my book reads 'I love you, but I never was romantically in love with you.' I feel this is even more desperate, because she never felt the love in the first place and she has given up."

Whatever way your wife words the message that she never really loved you, it is a horrible thing to hear. It seems to attack the very foundations of your marriage. However, there is one good thing about the declaration: it is out in the open. Once something like this has been said, rather than floating around in her head, it can be tested in the real world. Sometimes, the woman (or man) who says "I never loved you," will realize that this is an exaggeration. They did feel something when they walked down the aisle, not just the dramatic: can't sleep; can't eat; can't think of anything but you, from the movies. Sometimes, they will realize that they were depressed when they confessed and that made them exaggerate their feelings. Sometimes, they will realize what counts is right now—how you feel about each other today—rather than what happened 10 or 20 years ago.

So how do you help your wife from the bleakness of "I never really loved you," to something more nuanced and less desperate? I know you will want to debate what love really is or tell her that life isn't like the movies. However it will be much better to listen, ask questions to draw her out and really understand. Otherwise, you are on one side saying that there are more important things than romantic love (which might be true) while she is on the other side thinking that you are just not taking her seriously: "He's not interested in my feelings and therefore he's not interested in me." By all means, tell her what love means for you but respect her position and don't try and convince her that she is wrong.

Next, try to draw out what she means by "romantic love" or "truly in love." It is probably to do with feeling cherished and special. Hopefully, you're thinking "I can do that." In fact, if you've started to implement change, your goals will all revolve around cherishing your wife. In the spirit of better communication, tell her, "I want you to feel loved in this way," or "I would like the opportunity to protect you, to make you feel special, cherished and at the center of my life," or whatever words feel natural and real to you. Remember it does not have to be grand romantic gestures if she's not up for those at the moment, but listening to her and respecting her wants, needs and beliefs.

Finally, and this is the hardest part, don't take it so personally. I know: it is personal. She never romantically loved *you*! All right, you could have expressed your feelings more freely or been more thoughtful (and you're going to do something about that). However, she has to take responsibility too for holding her emotional cards close to her chest—either because she was frightened of getting hurt, did not expect love (because she received only qualified love as a child) or did not trust her own feelings (and let the green shoots of love grow into the jungle of emotions described in romantic books, songs and movies). If you can stop taking these comments personally—and think about them as much as *her* failings as your own—you will be less defensive, less likely to panic and more able to listen.

"It's too late" and "I can't change my feelings"

There is no ending to the depressing and seemingly hopeless statements that people who have fallen out of love make. It goes with the territory. However, by now, you will have realised that the picture is more complicated than these statements appear at first sight:

"What can I do? I really don't feel that I know my wife anymore as how she is behaving is totally out of character with what she's always said and done in the past. I almost feel that she is hiding something and if she could let it out, we could move on and resolve this together but I can't even get her to talk to me about it without her just falling back onto 'it's too late and I just know that I don't want you.'"

If your wife is holding something back, it is most likely to be criticism of you. In her head, she's thinking: "He's hurting enough without sticking in the knife too." That's fine but how can you address the issues if you don't really know the full extent of the problems? So here is how you draw her out:

First, choose your time rather than letting it all come pouring out in the middle of an argument—when anger and frustration will encourage her to exaggerate her criticism of your behavior and amplify her hurt.

Secondly, give her permission to be honest: "I would rather know so I can make an informed choice," or "I'm going to be imagining all sorts of horrible things," or "Better out than in."

Thirdly, keep calm and listen (hopefully without getting angry or tearful) and then report back your feelings: "I felt sad when you said . . ." In this way, she will treat you as an adult (that has a right to know) rather than a child (who she has to protect).

During this conversation, you are probably going to get "I can't change my feelings." It seems like another dead end because if her feelings don't change, she won't fall in love again and who wants to be in a loveless marriage? However feelings are not independent things that float around in the heart, they are based on events and thoughts. So while I never challenge my clients' feelings—because they know when they feel sad, angry or in love—I will challenge thoughts and how someone interprets an event. For example, you send your wife a chatty text. If she does not reply, you think: "She can't even be bothered to reply to a simple text. She can't love me." With this interpretation, your feelings will probably be despair. If you think: "Perhaps her phone is out of battery," or "She's left her phone at home again," then your feelings will be disappointment. So how can you use this knowledge to combat "I can't change my feelings"?

If you start to communicate better, there is less chance for your wife to interpret your behaviour as unloving and her feelings will begin to soften. If you provide more positive events—rather than getting angry thereby adding more negative ones to her list—the balance will begin to tip and she will view your relationship more positively. Finally, her feelings will start to become more loving.

What about, "it's too late" and "I don't know what I want"? These statements are only a problem if you are pressing for a decision at this precise moment. If, instead, you remember that this is the age of uncertainty and put off talking about the future, you can focus on improving your relationship today (and let tomorrow take care of itself).

Finally, whatever negatives your wife comes out with, try to thank her. After all, you have made a significant step forward. Your communication has improved. You have a better understanding of your relationship and how to resolve the problems. And most importantly, once you understand your wife's thought processes, you can make a better case for staying together. So openness and honesty—however tough to hear— is better than her clamming up and walking away.

Importance of "framing" your story

When it comes to who wins an argument, it is seldom the person with the best grasp of the facts, or the best debater but the one with the most convincing story. So how do you frame your current situation so it is not dominated by your wife's negative message: "I don't love you anymore," and allow your positive one: "We can turn this around," to be heard?

One idea comes from Professor Marshall Ganz who dropped out of Harvard to organise migrant workers in the 1960s and returned 30 years later to finish his degree and teach a new generation what he'd learned about motivating people and achieving change. At the core of his philosophy is the idea that you need to make your pitch in three parts:

> *Why you feel called to act (Story of Self)*
> *How this relates to the audience (Story of Us)*
> *What urgent challenge this action seeks*
> *   (Story of Now)*

The best example of its power comes from Barack Obama's speech to the 2004 Democratic Convention. At this point, he was just a little-known candidate for the US Senate. His speech not only electrified the audience but put him on the map and paved the way for becoming President just four years later. His story was incredibly simple:

> *I am the son of a Kenyan goat herder running for*
> *Senate (Self)*
> *I am a symbol of American meritocracy (Us)*
> *I am threatened by the elitist policies and cronyism*
> *of the Bush White House (Now)*

Of course, this story played well because Obama had "framed" it in a way guaranteed to resonate with his audience. The American Dream is built on the idea that anybody can rise to the top and Obama had cast himself as a living example: someone with no special privileges and from Hawaii, one of the smallest and most out of the way states. (A sharp contrast with George W. Bush, whose father had been President and who had every advantage money could buy.) Obama's audience were ordinary men and women too who were also struggling to get ahead and could readily identify with his ambitions. However, here is the clever part. By supporting Obama, they were effectively cheering themselves on. Obama's success proved that the American Dream worked (and by extension, that they too could climb to the top) and he was promising to take away the blocks that were holding them back (thereby doubling their chances). So how does this relate to your situation?

Your wife is currently framing the story in this way:

I've fallen out of love (Self)
Our marriage is fatally flawed (Us)
It would be better for everyone if we split up (Now)

Of course, there are variations on the themes. For "Us" it might be, "we are wrong for each other" or "we've tried before and nothing really changes" or "I don't think we can work this out." For "Now" it might be, "I want to find someone else before I'm too old" or "I'm exhausted by all the arguing and fights and can't carry on any longer."

Maybe your wife is framing the story in a different way but before you can start to combat it, you need to be clear what you're up against. So write down your wife's story to herself, you and the world. This should be reasonably easy as you've probably heard it a million times before.

Story of Self:
Story of Us:
Story of Now:

Next, write down your own story. Don't try and dress it up, just write the core of your message:

Story of Self:

Story of Us:
Story of Now:

Why your story is falling on deaf ears

Most husbands will put down, "I still love you" (or some variation on the theme) for "Self." I think there is a more convincing story but we'll come to that later. However, I have heard some really poor ones. For example: "I had a stroke five years ago/I've been struggling with depression," which sounds either weak: "Don't hurt me," or helpless: "I can't manage on my own," or accusing: "The stress might kill me," and "It's not fair after everything I've done for you," which simply sounds bitter. I've also heard some uninspiring stories of "Us." For example: "Don't expect marriages to be a bed of roses," or "You won't do any better."

If you're having trouble framing your story, think of it as a banner to march behind and something to put fire into your bellies to keep going through the tough times. Therefore your story must be positive and aspirational:

> *I've had a huge wake-up call (Self)*
> *I have to thank you for stopping me from drifting*
>   *(Us)*
> *With your bravery (of owning up to the problem)*
>   *and all my determination (the changes I'm*
>   *making), this is the chance to have a truly*
>   *fulfilling relationship (Now)*

Love Coach's Three Key Things
to Remember:

- This is the age of uncertainty. Use the time to implement change, prove that you are listening and that you value your wife's feelings (as this will make her feel valued).

- If there are setbacks, you need to acknowledge and learn from them rather than distracting yourself.

- Instead of trying to knock down your wife's negative story, take the initiative by framing the situation in a positive way.

Chapter Five

How do I know when it's best to give up and stop trying?

"We are now a few weeks into the separation and I am struggling to see the benefit. We talk on the phone once a week but not about anything to do with our problems particularly, and she becomes upset by hearing the sound of my voice. She says she is really suffering, but she won't come home. I am devastated but unable to let her go, as it feels like a tragedy, and that she is leaving for the wrong reasons. Our separation does not feel productive, nor can we work on anything together, and it's hard for me to work on myself as I am always wondering about her. I am at the end of my tether, but still love her deeply. Should I give up or fight till the bitter end?"

Although you don't really want to end your marriage, you're frightened of wasting even more time and emotional energy on a relationship that could be going nowhere. It feels like you're hitting your head against a brick wall, so perhaps you should bow to the inevitable? Except, the minute you consider the reality of life without your wife, you're swept away by a wave of despair. So you swing back to soldiering on, but the pain is so great you don't think this is a viable option either. If this dilemma sounds familiar, how do you cut through the confusion and make a decision one way or the other?

Five questions to help you find clarity

People who get stuck in the "should I give up or fight on" trap are looking at their relationship like a judge in rather black or white terms: "Guilty or not guilty," or more accurately "Over or not." However, in my experience, it is better to be like a doctor and make a diagnosis: "How healthy is this relationship and can it still be saved?"

Am I just temporarily down?

It could be that this is the worst time to decide if your relationship has a future. Perhaps you're tired (when everything seems worse), not been eating properly (because if your wife doesn't love you, you don't love yourself enough to look after yourself), stressed because of some extra pressure at work (previously you'd have been able to cope with her love and support) or it's around a significant holiday or anniversary (when you remember all the good times and worry about the future). Even if you think this may be a temporary down, don't ignore it. In the same way that I'm asking you to listen to your wife, I want you to listen to your own feelings too. Perhaps you need extra help: speak to your doctor, find more supporters or maybe take a short break away. Alternatively, you might need to give yourself a little TLC—maybe a long bath or an early night.

If, however, this down feeling is part of a pattern (for example, you talk yourself up and then crash, or concentrate all your energy on one particular rescue strategy and when it fails are faced with the full-scale of the problems), it could be that your relationship has gone past the point of no return. However, don't jump to any conclusion until you have looked at the rest of the questions.

Am I oversimplifying the situation?

When we examine our own motivations we come up with a multitude of interlocking reasons for our behavior—some positive, some defensive and some in-between. When we examine our own feelings, there are a complex set of competing emotions. At the moment, you can probably alternate between hope and despair, joy and misery, or anger and love. If someone asked how you've been feeling it would take about 15 minutes to explain and depend on which moment in the last few days that they are asking about. However, while we are ready to accept our own complexity, we tend to put our partner's motivations down to just one thing: "She doesn't love me," or "She wants to hurt me." Worse still, this can tip over into thinking that you know your wife's feelings and therefore can assume what is going on in her head: "This means she's moving on." If you're not careful, your assumption—which is built on smoke and mirrors—becomes your solid reality and you have talked yourself into giving up.

Next time you find yourself coming up with one overriding explanation for your wife's behavior or assuming that you can mind-read, tell yourself: "This is the age of uncertainty. I might hate not knowing but it is worse to guess and guess wrong. So let it drop for now."

If, however, you keep saying "yes but..." when you try to dis-engage your overactive mind, it could be that you have had enough and need to review whether you have the energy to continue. The next three questions will help you decide if this is the case.

Am I still growing?

It is every man's worst nightmare: "What if I put all this effort into saving my marriage and she throws it all back in my face?" Certainly, I wouldn't want you to endure all this pain and soul-searching for nothing. However, this program is not just about saving your marriage but learning about yourself and improving communication too. Obviously, the best outcome is that your wife falls back in love and you both live happily ever after. However, there are other outcomes worth having. If your marriage can't be saved but you and your wife learn to become better co-parents, it is worth pressing on (at least for now). Finally, if you are learning to be a better man, and to not make the same mistakes again, you will make someone else a wonderful husband and find lasting happiness.

So if you're still learning, improving communication, listening to other people and yourself, I think it is worth continuing the fight. The relationship is either healthy or you will find a healthy outcome, so press on.

If, however, you have already found a sort of peace between you and your wife (and you can cooperate over the children) or have taken all the lessons from this dismal situation you possibly can, then maybe you have your answer.

Have I really tried everything?

It might seem that you've explored all the possibilities but most people have simply used the same failed strategy over and over again—just bigger and bigger. For example, shouting louder or sulking for longer. So if there are still other strategies to try—and this book is full of them—it is worth fighting on. Even if your marriage is beyond saving, you will be able to tell yourself that you did all you could and that will help you feel less guilty and make a better recovery.

If, however, you have read this book, re-read it, tried all the strategies and still keeping coming up against a brick wall, you have another damning answer. But before you make up your mind, there is one final question (perhaps the most important one) and one more strategy (at the end of this chapter).

Do you have enough love to give without getting anything back—at least in the short term?

This fifth question is the key one. If you still love your wife enough to be compassionate for her feelings and can be generous enough to keep giving without getting anything back (for a little bit longer), there is still hope that your marriage can be saved.

If all you can think is: "After what she's done," or "After what she's said," or "Yes but she's got to . . ." then either it's too soon after a nasty discovery (and you're still in shock) or your marriage is truly over.

Hopefully, these five questions will have given you a lot to think about. If you're still uncertain, imagine your heart is like a cupboard. If you open the door and there is something left to feed your relationship, that's a good sign. If the cupboard is empty or it feels like you would have to cut off a pound of your own flesh, that's a bad sign. However, I'd like to think that just the fact that you've bought this book means that you still have enough love left and that means it's not too late.

My wife has turned into a different person

What if your wife says: "I've changed," or "I want different things," and sometimes you truly believe that aliens have stolen your wife and replaced her with a stranger? Under these circumstances, it's not surprising that you are full of despair and don't know what to do for the best.

"*I met my wife at our place of work when she was 17, but we didn't start our relationship until she was 21. I am now 40, my wife is 35 and we have two children. My wife never had a large circle of friends other than those at work and as a result never had much of a social life outside our joint friends. This changed when our youngest started school and my wife made some very good friends with other moms from school. In addition, she joined the PTA in order to support the school in other ways. She jumped in with both feet and was very keen and got involved with the organization of the group and their events. I was happy for her. She now had another focus outside of being a wife and mom, and had her own identity. During this time, my wife also became very conscious of her appearance and spent a lot of time at the gym. She lost weight, changed the way she dressed, changed her hair, and started going out a lot more. I was genuinely happy for her. Then without warning, five months ago she told me she loved me but wasn't in love anymore. She explained that she had been struggling with her feelings for about two years. She had contemplated different scenarios, different ways of getting the love back, but had found no solution, and the only option left was to split up. She was unable to explain 'why', and I couldn't understand. All she could say was, 'I don't know what I want,*

> *but I know I don't want you'. Many of our friends*
> *and family say she has changed, and they don't rec-*
> *ognize her anymore. We are 'the last couple [they]*
> *imagined this could happen to', and those that know*
> *her say they just don't understand."*

It is great to be childhood sweethearts and have been together forever. However, as people approach 40, they look back at the paths they didn't take. "What if I'd gone to college?" "What if I'd followed my ambitions to be a rock star?" "What if I'd seen a bit more of the world before I settled down?" This is a perfectly natural part of growing older and everybody goes through it but it is more acute for childhood sweethearts who have had less opportunity to experiment. Around the mid-point in our lives, we become more aware of our mortality—perhaps one of our parents dies—and we start to calculate how much time we've got left and what we want to do with it. During this soul-searching, everything is up for debate and this includes our relationships—especially in the following two scenarios.

Firstly, your wife finds your marriage disappointing because she hasn't felt special or cherished. If she falls into this category, I hope my book has already given you some strategies for combating the problem. Secondly, the two of you have been so close and done so much together that it is hard to work out where, for her, being a wife and mother ends and being a person in her own right begins. She asks herself: "Who am I?" "What do I want from life?" As I hope you're beginning to realize, these are very difficult questions to answer and many people shy away from them. We want simple and easy solutions. So many women go to the gym (to change the way they look) or go out more (to have a bit of fun). Alternatively, some women (and men too) are frightened of looking too deeply for fear of what they might find and the impact on the family. What if they do a lot of soul-searching and discover they are deeply unhappy, can't be themselves or that their husbands are stopping them from achieving their goals? Unfortunately, suppressing these thoughts doesn't make them go away but instead they multiply until the wives confess: "I don't love you anymore," and "You're holding me back." For many husbands, this is a complete shock. They haven't prevented their wife doing anything. In fact, they have positively encouraged her to go out with her friends or been happy to babysit.

So if your wife has become a stranger or seems to be going through a mid-life crisis, what should you do?

Embrace change

We don't like change. It is uncomfortable, scary and we do our best to avoid it. "What if we grow apart?" "What if she changes and wants different things?" "What if she wants me to be the sort of man I can't be?" It is easy to catastrophize and imagine that this is the end of your relationship but while you are panicking, it is easy to overlook the upside. It would be a dull world if we were exactly the same at 17 and 47. It might feel comfortable to know someone inside out or be able to predict the way they will react but it is also incredibly boring.

What's more, "possessing" someone kills passion: after all we desire what we haven't got—or at least what we don't feel 100 percent sure of. (I bet that since your wife has threatened to leave, your interest in her has sky-rocketed!)

It is good, from time to time, to audit your life and put everything up for discussion. The problem is when some subjects are off-limits—like your relationship. As I've explained before, negative thoughts are better out than in, so they can be tested in the real world. Anything that is suppressed and unmentionable gains power and becomes even scarier in the shadows.

So thank your wife for being honest and explain how her soul-searching has encouraged you to do something similar and tell her what you would like to change about yourself.

Be honest with yourself

Going back to the previous idea of imagining everything your wife says is true—at least from her perspective—have you truly supported her changes? Have you agreed to babysit but grudgingly, so your wife felt she could only ask occasionally? Although you haven't banned her from going out, have you used more subtle ways of getting your way—for example, sighing or saying "out again?" or being passive aggressive (not leaving work on time, so you're back late and she misses the first part of her class)? Maybe you've appealed to her better judgment: "We're happier just the two of us," or "Don't go because you'll never find anywhere to park." Perhaps you've just assumed: "We like a nice quiet weekend at home," or "We don't like noisy clubs or pubs," and not actually checked out whether your wife agrees or not. If any of these strike a chord, make a fulsome apology.

Become part of the change

If you genuinely believe that you have supported your wife, try going the extra mile. For example, help set up the refreshments tent for her PTA fundraiser or suggest inviting the members of her choir and their partners over for a barbecue. In this way, you will begin to know some of the personalities involved and, even better, when she needs help she knows she can count on you. If she is taking a course, go along to the orientation or read a set text so that you can intelligently discuss her interest. Alternatively, you could volunteer for childcare when she can't find anybody else—especially if you have a demanding job. I can't tell you how often counseling is turned around by a husband taking an afternoon's leave to solve a childcare crisis. Many men don't realize just how much energy their wife puts into thinking about who will look after the children (and maybe the dog too). If you show that you understand how her life works and will try to be flexible, you will be part of her support team (rather than somebody else whose needs she must accommodate).

Follow the program

Although it feels deeply personal: "I don't know what I want but I don't want you," don't let your panic stop you from working on your communication skills, becoming more assertive and a better listener. What your wife is saying is: "I don't want my old life," and that's fine because circumstances change and life changes us. She is not necessarily saying: "I don't want you," rather "I don't want the same old you." And again, that's fine because you can change and grow too.

Temporary Separations

What if your wife is asking for space or has already moved out? Can you still work on your marriage? The future might seem bleak but that doesn't mean you can't salvage the situation.

> "My wife keeps crying. She says she's sick of talking about us. I just wanted to know, 'what are we doing?' and she said to 'just stay separated'. She will contact me when she wants something or to do something. So now I feel like I hold zero cards. The decision of 'us' is completely in her hands unless I move on, which I can't fathom I would. I love her."

I'm not a great fan of temporary separations, because I want the two of you to communicate better and being apart means fewer opportunities to interact. I also don't believe in the idea of "if I'm away from you, perhaps I'll miss you and want to be with you again." The problems are too deep-rooted for something so straightforward.

Avoiding a temporary separation

Most couples facing "I love you but . . ." will talk about a temporary separation at some point. So how should you respond? On one hand, I want you to listen to your wife (if she needs time out) but on the other, I discourage temporary separations as it makes it harder to save your marriage (and you've got enough problems already). I know these two statements contradict each other.

The solution is to look for a middle way, where your wife has space but you can still work on your marriage. In many ways, this discussion is a great place to start improving communication. Can you express your different opinions, listen (without trying to talk each other down) and then negotiate? Perhaps one of the following middle ways might be the solution (but don't suggest them until you have truly heard your wife's wants, needs and beliefs):

Have a few days away. This will give you both a chance to step back, calm down and think everything through. It will not be a magic solution but it could allow some fresh insights and for each of you to be rested enough to interact better. It could be that your wife would like to visit a friend (and have time without the children) or it could be that you should go away.

Give her psychological space. By this I mean stop pressuring, checking up on her and asking for reassurance. If you've just bought this book, explain what you've learned so far and ask for the opportunity to try stepping back. In addition, give her permission to tell you if something feels like you're invading her psychological space and commit to not getting defensive or angry. Finally, agree to review the situation in two weeks' time and assess whether psychological space is enough.

Move into the spare room. If you haven't got enough room, you could possibly suggest sleeping on the sofa or buying a sofa bed. This is especially useful if you find it hard not to pressure her for "make-up" sex or either one of you is finding it hard to sleep.

If your discussions reach an impasse or you have tried these intermediate strategies for time out and they were not enough, I would suggest agreeing to a temporary separation. You might feel that you have no cards left but it is better to give in with good grace. It will also put you in a stronger position for what comes next.

Negotiating a temporary separation

Once again, this is another opportunity to improve your communication. So although this might feel like your darkest moment, it could also be the beginning of your fight back. Handled well, your wife could come away thinking: "He really listened to me," or "He didn't get angry or tearful, so perhaps he really can change," or "He's not so bad after all." Here are a few topics to discuss:

How long? Your wife will have no idea how much time she needs but it will be easier for you if the temporary separation is not open-ended. So ask for a review to be built in after one, two or three months. You can always extend the temporary separation but this way you will both know where you stand.

How often will you meet? Will you have occasional date nights or only see each other at social situations like friends' parties? Perhaps, it will be a complete break for a while? Talk about all the options. It could be that a date night might make you feel judged and you just want to meet for coffee and exchange mail. On these occasions, will you talk about "us" or keep it light?

What communication is acceptable? How often will you speak, text or email? What would feel comfortable and provide the chance to interact better—without deluging your wife with anxious messages?

What if there is an emergency? Perhaps one of your children is ill or your mother has an accident. Discuss what happens under these circumstances and what constitutes an emergency.

What about other people? Is it acceptable to see other men and women during your temporary separation? What do you say to the children? What do you tell friends? Talk through everything and spell out the ground rules, thereby avoiding any assumptions or miscommunication.

Coping with a temporary separation

If day-to-day life has become incredibly stressful and something as simple as "have you seen my keys?" triggers a quarrel or your fights have become destructive, time apart can help you return from the edge, calm down and find enough good-will to try again. A temporary separation does not necessarily have to lead to a permanent separation, if you follow these guidelines:

Focus on eliminating misunderstandings. When communicating at a distance, without the benefit of body language, a smile or the tone of voice to soften a message, most couples end up misunderstanding each other. So try and keep email and texts on a businesslike basis: "What time should I pick up the kids?" "How many packed lunches should I bring?" Keep emotionally charged matters for a face-to-face conversation or, at the very least, on the phone. If you get an upsetting text or email from your wife, don't reply right away. It might be that you have jumped to the wrong conclusion. Even if she has indeed sent an angry message, it is not helpful to send one back. Remember the importance of acknowledging—even in emails and texts: "I know you are angry but..." and then reply in as neutral a way as possible. For example: "I know you're angry but can we discuss this when we meet on Wednesday?" If you must communicate something important by email, write a draft and leave it for at least 24 hours before sending it. The next day, it might not seem so important or you might decide to tone down the language.

Make certain that you are truly giving her space. I have worked with some men who besieged their wives (and her friends and family) with texts, emails and calls during a temporary separation. In some cases, it took a lot of work to get them down to just one email a day. I know you are going to be worrying that you are out of sight, out of mind and I know you want to know that she got home safely and that issues like: "What shall we do about my cousin's wedding next month?" seem incredibly pressing. However, be honest with yourself. Are you using this minimal contact to keep a lid on your panic? Unfortunately, you are also putting yourself in the worst of all worlds: a temporary separation that does not feel like one to your wife. She is in danger of thinking: "If I'm going to get any space and time to myself without him constantly tugging at my sleeve I need to end this relationship." If this sounds familiar, go back through the book and find another way of dealing with your panic. You might also find that a little less contact—and worrying about why she has not replied to your thirtieth text—will help you feel calmer and better able to cope. Even if you are doubtful, please experiment with cutting down the number of messages for a few days and review the impact on your relationship and your sanity.

Focus on looking after yourself. Use the time apart as an opportunity to cherish yourself. By this I mean improving your diet, reducing your alcohol intake, getting some more exercise—but most importantly—giving yourself an occasional small treat. For example, spending an extra half hour in bed and going into work late or going on a day's fishing trip. I find that some men can't cherish their wives because they have nothing to give. It is almost as if a little voice inside is saying:

"What about me?" If you can be kind and generous to yourself, you will find it easier to extend the same compassion to your wife.

Don't use a temporary separation as an excuse for doing nothing. Of course, the strategies in this book are easier with regular face-to-face contact, but you can still concentrate on making your limited contact better and start working on yourself.

Be as real as possible. How do you behave when you meet up? Should you concentrate on enjoying yourself (although that can seem like sweeping problems under the carpet) or should you have serious conversations (except that can seem like you never have any fun)? Rather than opting for light or heavy, I would like you to be real. For example, go out for a drink and enjoy yourself but if something comes up then talk about it. If you feel like you're walking on eggshells, ask her why or acknowledge what's happening: "You seem upset that I want to go home now." If it's you who's upset, tell her why: "I wonder if you're just meeting up in order to check the box rather than letting go and enjoying yourself." Even if it creates a moment of unpleasantness, that's better than the alternative (which many couples use) of firing off an angry text after the date. Not only is it too late to change plans—for example, having a coffee before heading home—but you've wasted an opportunity to communicate better. By being real, you can enjoy yourself, still work on the relationship when necessary but, most importantly, make the best of your time together.

I think my wife might be having an affair

What if the situation is even worse: your wife has not moved out but seems to have emotionally left and has started looking for another relationship?

> *"I recently discovered my wife has been on a dating website and emailed and exchanged texts with at least two men. She doesn't know I found out (she left herself logged into her email account by mistake) and I haven't confronted her. I also saw that she has been looking at smaller properties in the area for herself. Is it too late to save our relationship?"*

Emails, texts and computer searches leave a trail that is easy to follow. With a little detective work, you can probably reveal all sorts of dark secrets. But will it help save your marriage? On one hand, you want to know where you stand (and could potentially head off an affair) but on the other, you will be infringing your wife's privacy and risking the accusation of checking up on her or being controlling. Instead of the focus being on how to save your marriage, you are discussing whether your wife is too close with someone at work, when being friendly tips over into flirting, what constitutes cheating and what is harmless fun. Worse still, you are on opposite sides rather than working as a team.

If you are concerned about another man, it is better to ask rather than go looking for evidence. You are more likely to get a straight answer if you are calm rather than making accusations during a quarrel. Below are four questions to elicit information and if they don't work, I have added three invitations to confess:

- Have you been talking about our problems to another man?

- Has someone been more than just a friend?

- Have you been flirting online or texting another man?

- Why have you been secretive about your phone/email passwords/switched screens when I've come into the room?

- I would rather know the truth, however painful, and understand the full extent of the problem, than be left in the dark.

- I promise I won't get angry and I'll listen quietly to your explanations.

- It will hurt me even more if I find out at a later date that you have not been honest with me.

If you do come across incriminating evidence, it is better to come clean and tell your wife. Otherwise, your feelings will leak out as snide comments and general bitterness or you will appear distant and angry. Be wary of dumping all your anger on this other man as this will encourage your wife to defend him. I have counseled men who have phoned their rival's boss and got him sacked. The majority regretted their decisions because it pushed the lovers closer together and turned the aggrieved husband into the villain and the other man into the victim. Equally disastrous, but harder to avoid, is obsessing about him. It is easy to think: "If only he wasn't here, then we could solve our problems," or "He's the obstacle," but that is focusing on the symptoms, rather than the underlying problems. Most women who form inappropriate friendships that cross over into affairs do so because they are deeply unhappy at home, feel unheard or unappreciated. Although, it is natural to be hurt, angry and rejected, it is better to focus on *why* your wife was tempted rather than *what* she has been doing. So please still follow the general advice and concentrate on listening, asking questions and trying to stand in your wife's shoes.

My wife is in love with someone else

Most affairs end shortly after they've been discovered. The partner who has been unfaithful realizes how stupid they have been, wonder how they could have put their marriage in such jeopardy and commit to saving their marriage. Unfortunately, there are some women who feel torn between their loyalty to their husband and their feelings for their affair partner. Without doubt, this is the bleakest scenario of all and needs very careful handling.

> *"I have been with my wife for six years (married for one and a half) and she recently had an affair with a work colleague that lasted six months. She recognizes she has made a mistake and can't be friends with her lover anymore but she is struggling to let go of him. This is getting in the way of our healing process. I think I am trying to compare myself to her lover as for her things*

were exciting as they were fresh and passionate. But my wife and I had moved past that into a more mature and deep love and it seems my wife was lacking some desire for me. I just want to get it back."

If this is your situation, you have my commiserations. It will feel like you're going mad. You can't sit still, concentrate on work or even think straight: "What is she up to?" "What if she's talking to him?" "She could be kissing him right now." You will do literally *anything* to win her back. And this is the problem!

Before I explain your options, it is important to remember that the vast majority of affairs do not translate into lasting relationships. So although you fear that your wife will walk into the sunset arm in arm with her new lover—leaving you with sand kicked in your face—the odds of this happening are small. So what should you do? Start by *not* comparing yourself to her lover. Partly because you'll be comparing your fantasy of him with the darkest and most critical version you can muster of yourself, but mainly because comparing the bubble of an affair with committed love is like comparing a bag of chips with a home-cooked meal. Sure the chips are convenient, readily available and tasty but it is all salt, additives, bright packaging and empty calories. It does not truly feed you.

If she decides to stay

If your wife has decided that she wants to save your marriage, she will need to grieve for what she has lost before she can accept your love again. This does not stop you from improving everyday communication, understanding why your relationship reached this point and beginning to make changes yourself. (However, don't expect too much in return from your wife just yet.) In an ideal world, you would agree not to keep checking on her—reading her emails, pretending to phone for a chat but really to find out what she's doing, or pushing for reassurance—and she would agree to forward any new texts or emails from the other man and report any telephone calls. However, from long experience, I know this is very difficult. Even wives who are committed to saving their marriage will put off telling about a call—perhaps because they don't want to spoil a family day out with a quarrel—and get caught out by their husband. Equally, the most sensible husbands will have a moment of madness where, for example, they will tamper with the address book on their wife's phone so if she texts the other man it will come through to a secret number he has set up. When you do fail to keep the full disclosure/no checking up pledge, please apologize but accept that any slip is more to do with human frailty and stupidity rather than your darkest fears: "She will never love me," or "This proves that she can't let him go." Remember, it takes time to end a relationship. There will be times when she is thinking about him (that's a natural part of letting go); it does not necessarily mean that she wants to end her marriage.

If she can't make up her mind

Breaking up a loving family is a huge decision for a woman but abandoning the "love" and "craving" for the other man is equally difficult. So what should you do if you're caught in no man's land where your wife is not seeing her lover but she doesn't see any future for your marriage either?

"My wife has been having an on/off affair for two years with our children's piano teacher who is six years younger, divorced and does not have children. This is clearly the most painful experience of my life. Behind the scenes close friends and family are quietly saying to my wife that her affair relationship is unreal, and to think very carefully about what she chooses to do. My wife's response is, 'they are not me'. She is having a cooling off period from the third party, which she admits is very difficult. She has considered leaving me for this man previously but has not taken that step. At the moment, she is confused, uncertain and deciding between: 1. Life on her own with our children. 2. Life on her own with our children that may include the third party continuing as a friend/lover away from the children initially, but potentially introducing him to them, friends and family at a later stage and 3. Staying within our marriage but this option seems poor in comparison. I am her best friend, and a wonderful father, but she is not attracted to me sexually: indeed has not been sexually attracted to me for many years (but our youngest is only six years old). She states that if we remain married, I would be settling for second best, and she questioned my self-respect for not choosing to

divorce her. I have said that my priority is our children at this time. I do not wish to separate/divorce and would wish that our marriage endures and that we all emerge happier. My wife says that without any sexual aspect to the marriage, there is no marriage and she repeats that she does not find me sexually attractive and cannot see this changing."

One minute you're in despair (she seems too far away and the road to recovery seems so tough) and the next she makes some kind gesture (like a smile or squeezing your hand) and suddenly there's a ray of hope. So what should you do?

- Do not try to "sell" your relationship to her. Nobody likes high-pressure salesmen; we would much rather choose for ourselves.

- Follow my program and improve communication.

- If you have been Mr. Nice Guy and swallowing your feelings, please start reporting them: "I feel angry when you...'

- When the topic of the future comes up, don't keep stressing "duty" or "family" as this puts you on one side (talking sense) and your wife on the other (talking about feelings). Instead talk about the loving and sexual connection that you both want to regain.

- Commit to changing your approach to sex (rather than expecting her to rekindle her desire). Men generally fall into one of the following traps: They pester for sex or they don't do enough groundwork before asking (i.e. casual touching during the day, compliments and making her feel special). Alternatively, they can be too rough in bed or so polite the lovemaking seems passionless. I cover how to get the sexual spark back in my book, *Have the Sex You Want. A Couple's Guide to Getting Back the Spark*.

- Try to focus on the next few days. Thinking too far into the future will only make you panic.

If she keeps changing her mind

What if it is *truly* the worst option: she can't choose between you and the other man? One week she wants to be with you, the next she can't forget him and has left home. However, she's hardly closed the door when she's texting you and wondering if she's made the biggest mistake of her life. Alternatively, she might be currently under your roof but it feels like you're sitting on a time bomb because he's bombarding her with messages and turning up at her workplace. This is when "I'll do anything to save my marriage," becomes a real problem. You will take her back—no questions asked. You will agree to any conditions—no matter that they make your blood run cold. You lose all respect for yourself—because you feel weak and helpless. You can't trust your wife or her love for you because rather than having to prove her commitment, you took her back, no questions asked. But worst of all, you risk doing lasting damage to your love that is hard to repair—even after the other man has disappeared off the scene.

So what should you do? I know you will hate this idea but I'm going to suggest it anyway. Step back and let her go. Affairs happen in a bubble and once they have been found out and the drama of coming and going is over, they deflate and the reality of cheating and the flaws of the other man are exposed. In the meantime, you can begin to get your head back together and make sensible plans for the future. It does not mean giving up hope but having reasonable conditions for accepting your wife back. For example, she goes to live with a female friend, her mother or takes an appartment on her own so she can be sure she is coming back for the right reasons: She loves you, respects you and wants to repair your marriage.

The final strategy

What if you've tried everything in my book and, although it has improved relations between the two of you, your wife still says she has to be true to herself or find a real connection or she believes that: "If we were truly meant to be together it wouldn't be so hard." Sometimes all the sensible advice from friends and family, hard work from husbands and the wisdom of experts, falls on deaf ears. She wants a soul mate; to click with someone and nothing will shake her conviction. Maybe even a small sane part of her knows that her plans are doomed but she feels she has to go for it anyway.

If this is the situation, you've got two choices. Neither of them is very pleasant. Firstly, you can make it as hard as possible for her, be bitter and angry and become the enemy. This will close the door forever. Or, secondly, you can let her go with your blessing and remain on reasonable terms. This will leave the door ajar. My hope is that she will discover that the grass is not really that green. The dating world is a jungle and love needs skill and not just connection. If you are still a friend, she might decide to talk over her problems, explain her feelings and begin to reassess your relationship.

So if you decide to bow to the inevitable and let her go, how should you play it?

- Continue to be assertive, listen and communicate honestly with your wife but don't be drawn into pointless quarrels.

- Work on yourself, learn about relationships and become the best version of yourself possible.

- Have firm boundaries between what is acceptable and unacceptable behavior and don't cross them.

- Don't play games. Some people will suggest going out on dates to make your wife jealous and get her to come running back. However, I don't think that is fair on your date. I don't think it is fair on your marriage either. Your future needs to be built on something more solid than tricking your wife into loving you.

- There's nothing wrong with seeing other people, as long as you explain your circumstances. It could help you reassess your marriage or confirm your decision to hold on, either way you will have a better understanding of your feelings.

- Bring new things into your life. Instead of getting depressed about the empty weekends, try activities you've never had time for before. For example, take a diving course or run a marathon. Not only will it make you feel better but what is going to be more intriguing for your wife: someone out doing interesting things or someone sitting at home and moping?

- Reassess after six months. This is six months from your decision to let her go rather than her telling you she doesn't love you anymore as this will give your wife enough time to sample the outside world. If she is still determined to press on with her new life, you will need to start to heal and move on. However, you will have learned a lot about yourself; you will have grown and become stronger. Under these circumstances no experience, however horrible, is ever wasted.

Don't panic!

I want to finish the book in the same way that I started it, by offering reassurance. You can turn your relationship around and get back the loving feelings. However, there will be setbacks and times when it feels you're taking one step forward and two back. Don't beat yourself up but instead learn from what went wrong, so you can avoid that pitfall next time around.

Of course, you want this problem sorted and to stop hurting. However, you have the whole of your life in front of you. In the greater scheme of things, does it matter if it takes a few months to resolve the issues? Most people mess up their marriage by ignoring problems—sometimes for years on end—and then when things come to a head, destroy it by wanting an answer or to know where they stand almost immediately. So why not try flipping this around and put some urgency into facing the problems while taking your time in finding a way forward? After all, there is no ticking clock.

Remember this is the age of uncertainty, so don't push for reassurance, bring up the future or ask about her feelings. Wait for your wife to raise these topics. Even when it seems your relationship has turned the corner, it will take a couple of months of "normal" for your wife to start to believe in you and her again. So please be patient and understanding and, most important, loving.

Love Coach's Three Key Things
to Remember:

- The true test of whether to give up or fight on is whether you can still give, even if you're not getting anything back.

- Temporary separations are best avoided but if one becomes inevitable, accept the situation and negotiate terms that increase the chances of saving your marriage.

- Sometimes it is best to make a tactical withdrawal rather than risk damaging your love for your wife.

Appendix

- Relationships are turned around by facing and solving small everyday issues.

- Don't swallow your needs, wants and opinions and don't pressure your wife to do the same either.

- Avoid focusing on your wife's genitals and breasts so you don't make her feel that you just want sex rather than to make love to all of her.

- This is the age of uncertainty. Use the time to implement change, prove that you are listening and that you value your wife's feelings (as this will make her feel valued).

- If there are setbacks, you need to acknowledge and learn from them rather than distracting yourself.

- Instead of trying to knock down your wife's negative story, take the initiative by framing the situation in a positive way.

- The true test of whether to give up or fight on is whether you can still give, even if you're not getting anything back.

- Temporary separations are best avoided but if one becomes inevitable, accept the situation and negotiate terms that increase the chances of saving your marriage.

- Sometimes it is best to make a tactical withdrawal rather than risk damaging your love for your wife.

Recommended Reading

By the Author

I Love You But I'm Not In Love With You: Seven Steps to Saving Your Relationship
This explains why love changes and how to get back the loving feelings. Essential reading alongside this book.

Help Your Partner Say Yes: Seven Steps to Achieving Better Cooperation and Communication
Learn why people find it so hard to change and how to ask in a clear and effective way.

Resolve Your Differences: Seven Steps to Dealing With Conflict in Your Relationship
There is more in this book about assertiveness and how to stop arguments growing toxic. (The chapter on low conflict relationships uses exercises and case histories from *I Love You But I'm Not in Love With You*).

Have the Sex You Want: A couple's guide to getting back the spark
How to re-establish chemistry with your wife and let the love flow between you. It is particularly helpful for couples with two children under five.

How can I ever trust you again? Infidelity: From discovery to recovery in seven steps
This book explains why affairs happen, how to stop your imagination going into over drive and why some couples get blocked in the recovery process.

Learn to love yourself enough: Seven steps to improving self-esteem in all your relationships
Everything you need to know to start working on yourself and repairing your battered self-confidence.

By others

At My Father's Wedding, John Lee
Explains why men find it hard to get in touch with their feelings and examines the complexity of father and son relationships.

What it is Like to Go to War, Karl Marlantes
Although this book is primarily about Marlantes time as a soldier in Vietnam, it is also about men and how we respond to intense pressure.

The Survivor Personality: How to Thrive and Survive in Any Life Crisis, Dr. Al Siebert
Includes how to be positive around negative people.

The Heart of the Buddha's Teaching, Thich Nhat Hanh
How to be mindful and live in the moment rather than worrying about the future.

Teach Us to Sit Still: A Sceptics Search for Health and Healing, Tim Parks
When faced with health problems that doctors could not explain or relieve, Parks sets off on a journey of personal discovery. Funny as well as thought provoking.

The Road Less Travelled, M. Scott Peck
A self-help classic which explains how avoiding pain only brings greater pain and explores the link between psychology and spirituality.

About the Author

Andrew G Marshall is a marital therapist and the author of the following books:

I Love You But I'm Not In Love With You: Seven Steps to Saving Your Relationship

How Can I Ever Trust You Again?: Infidelity: From Discovery to Recovery in Seven Steps

Are You Right for Me?: Seven Steps to Getting Clarity and Commitment in Your Relationship

Heal and Move On: Seven Steps to Recovering from a Break-up

Help Your Partner Say Yes: Seven Steps to Achieving Better Cooperation and Communication

Learn to Love Yourself Enough: Seven Steps to Improving Your Self-Esteem and Your Relationships

Resolve Your Differences: Seven Steps to Dealing With Conflict in Your Relationship

I Love You But You Always Put Me Last: Why The Kids-First Approach to Parenting Is Hurting Your Marriage—And the Proven Plan to Restore Balance

My Husband Doesn't Love Me and He's Texting Someone Else: The Love Coach Guide to Winning Him Back

What Is Love? 50 Questions About How to Find, Keep, and Rediscover It

Andrew trained with RELATE (the UK's leading couple's counselling charity) and has a private practice in London offering therapy, workshops and inspirational talks. He was the first UK-based therapist to have his work published by HCI Books (home of the famous Chicken Soup series) in the US. His books have been translated into over fifteen different languages and published in women's magazines all over the world. In the UK, he writes for the *Daily Mail* and *Mail on Sunday* newspapers.

More information about Andrew, the Marshall Method and coaching for winning back your wife can be found at:

www.andrewgmarshall.com